W9-AQD-341

Women in Antiquity:
An Annotated Bibliography

by

Leanna Goodwater

The Scarecrow Press, Inc.
Metuchen, N.J. 1975

Library of Congress Cataloging in Publication Data

Goodwater, Leanna, 1950-
Women in antiquity.

Includes indexes.
1. Women--Greece--Bibliography. 2. Women--Rome--Bibliography. 3. Women authors--Bibliography. I. Title.
Z7961.G66 [HQ1127] 016.30141'2'0938 75-23229
ISBN 0-8108-0837-4

Printed in the United States of America

CONTENTS

ACKNOWLEDGMENTS

For his guidance as this work took shape I am indebted to Dr. Stuart Baillie, professor of librarianship at San Jose State University. I would also like to thank Mr. Kenneth Fleissner and Mr. Michael Tillotson, teachers of classics at San Jose State, for their encouragement and valuable suggestions. I am especially grateful to the hard-worked pages at the main library of the University of California at Berkeley, who were kept busy running after many an obscure title for me. Finally, I would like to dedicate this book to my parents, without whom it would not have been possible.

L. G.

I

INTRODUCTION

Sir Henry Maine, the great nineteenth-century scholar, once said that "except the blind forces of nature, nothing moves in this world which is not Greek in its origin."[1] The student of Western civilization, after allowing for some exaggeration, is forced to agree. The legacy of Greece and Rome is with us today and permeates our whole existence; our customs, our institutions, our laws, our literature, our very thoughts owe a great debt to the ancients, and the same problems that plague us today were faced by them over two thousand years ago. Not the least among these was the fate and treatment of women.

Interest in this subject has seen a great revival in recent years after a long period of dormancy. With the onset of the women's liberation movement and the proliferation of academic women's studies programs, women are once more seriously examining their place in society and questioning their prescribed roles with an intensity equalled only during the years of the suffrage movement. There is a regrettable tendency, though, to begin the study of woman's history with her struggle for the vote, or to concentrate solely on her experiences in America, as though the history of woman somehow began a century ago on this side of the Atlantic. Many feminists, moreover, prefer to concentrate on the present and on future reforms. The future, and what we can make of it, is rightly our major concern, but it should not obscure the lesson of the old truism, that you can't tell where you're going if you don't know where you've been. To know what we can achieve in the future we must come to grips with what we have been able to achieve in the past, and in our society, so strongly influenced by the Greeks and Romans, an understanding of woman's place amongst them takes on special significance.

One of the first questions the feminist must deal with is whether or not woman has always been subject to patriarchal authority. Certainly no matriarchy--or even a state of true equality--has ever existed in recorded history, but of the dim ages of prehistory no one can be certain. Early civilizations preceded the classical Greeks and Romans: mysterious cultures of Minoans, Etruscans, and others, whose artifacts suggest a higher position for women than in later times. The Lycians of Asia Minor, for example, traced their descent on their mother's side, as Herodotus reports, calling each other by their mother's name.[2] The matronymic was prominent also among the Etruscans, and, as one scholar has noted, "Etruscan civilization was an archaic civilization. Its feminism, strange as it may seem to us, is not so much a recent conquest as a distant survival threatened by Graeco-Roman pressures; it recalls in many respects the Crete of Ariadne and the paintings of Cnossos."[3] Many prominent scholars (notably J. J. Bachofen, Robert Briffault, and Jane Ellen Harrison) have concluded from their extensive studies of archaeology and myth that these first civilizations were actually matriarchal but were overwhelmed and destroyed by a patriarchal revolution sometime before the dawn of history. Their conclusions, more recently espoused by the influential feminists, Helen Diner and Elizabeth Gould Davis, are still hotly debated by more traditional scholars. One may not go so far as to agree with Ms. Davis that women originated all civilization, invented all the crafts, and "dragged man, kicking and screaming, out of savagery," but the implications of ancient customs and religious practices, archaeology and anthropology, can not be dismissed lightly.[4]

With the advent of written history, though, we step on more solid ground. Women emerge from the darkness of prehistory in the epics of Homer, where they often play an important role. The Odyssey is especially noteworthy for its remarkable women: spirited young Nausicaa, powerful Calypso and Circe, Arete and Helen, who run their households with little male interference, and, of course, clever Penelope. So important are these women, and so strongly does the plot revolve around their actions, that Samuel Butler felt convinced that a woman must have composed the poem; he even wrote a book, The Authoress of the Odyssey, to prove it. With the Iliad, now, the case is different. Being concerned with war and battles, it is strongly a man's poem, yet it offers brief, sympathetic glimpses of woman's lot. The evidence of the poems indicates that women held a far higher social position in the Homeric period than at any other time in Greek history. They were not confined to the home, but moved freely in society and shared at times in the serious discourse of the men. Says one author,

> The woman was honored for her useful role in the economy, for her talents as an arbiter of disputes, for her importance as a mother whose children will carry on the family name, as the faithful and devoted consort of a great warrior, the preserver of morality and tradition.[5]

Between the Homeric poems and the next works of

Greek literature intervenes a gap of centuries, during which the position of women went into a sharp decline, apparently reaching its lowest point in fifth-century Athens. Women, especially married women, vanish from Greek history. In Herodotus woman is everywhere, so much so that a prominent scholar once summarized his approach to history as "cherchez la femme et n'oubliez pas le Dieu."[6] But in Thucydides woman is nowhere to be seen. His standard of feminine excellence is summed up in the words he attributes to Pericles in his famous funeral oration: "Great will be your glory in not falling short of your natural character; and greatest will be hers who is least talked of among the men whether for good or for bad."[7] This glory the Athenian woman certainly attained, for, though Athens was blessed with more great thinkers, artists, and writers than any other single city in history, "not one Athenian woman ever attained to the slightest distinction in any one department of literature, art, or science."[8]

That the Greek woman was not deficient in ability is made clear by the achievements of the women poets who lived at an earlier time. Pre-eminent among these was, of course, Sappho, one of the greatest lyric poets of all time, who apparently ran some sort of salon or boarding school for young girls on the island of Lesbos around 600 B.C. Of the nine books of her poems which the Alexandrian Library once possessed, a wretchedly small number of fragments remain; only two poems are in a state even approaching completeness. Yet her genius shines through them so brightly that her position remains unchallenged. Plato hailed her as the Tenth Muse, and C. M. Bowra summed up his views as follows:

> Her words are as fresh today as when she wrote them, and though we have only a pathetically small portion of what she wrote, and much even of this has survived for reasons other than its poetical merits, she still deserves the reputation of being the most gifted woman who ever wrote poetry. Her unfailing senses, her delightful fancy, her scrupulous sincerity, her passionate strength, even her outbursts of anger or scorn, are the qualities of a character endowed beyond mortal measure by the Muses and the Graces.[9]

For the first time in history we hear the voice of a woman speaking about and for her sex, and it is surely a voice worthy to be heard.

Sappho was unique in the ancient world, but she did not stand alone. She had talented successors--Corinna, who defeated Pindar five times in the lyric competitions at Thebes, Erinna of Telos, Praxilla, and Telesilla, as well as other minor poetesses: Anyte of Tegea, Charixena, Cleobuline Melinno, Moero, Myrtis, and Nossis. Paltry as the remains of their works are, they provide a much-needed relief to the blatant misogyny which dominates much of classical literature.

Why woman's status declined after Homer's time is unknown. Increased contact with the cities of Asia Minor may have caused strong oriental influences to alter Greek culture; certainly, the restricted life of women in Periclean Athens has often been labeled "Oriental seclusion." A girl's marriage was arranged for her by her father, often when she was only about fifteen, to a bridegroom several years older whom she may never have seen before. Up to that time she had "lived under the most cramping restrictions, trained from childhood to see and hear as little as possible, and ask an absolute minimum of questions."[10] Her mother had taught her the necessary domestic skills, maybe a little reading if she was lucky, and little else; such was considered a good education for a girl. After marriage her life was no freer. She was confined to the gynaeceum, or women's apartments, and was allowed to venture forth with propriety only during religious festivals or for special family events. She could not own property or conduct legal business, nor could she attend the assembly or (some claim) the theatre; from birth to death she was the legal ward of her father, husband, or nearest male relative. Only in the home did she have any authority.

With such limited experience, education, and mental horizon, is it any wonder that Athenian women were often nonentities, whose very names are lost to the ken of history? The Athenian men, caught up in a world of intellectual and political excitement, could hardly turn to their wives for mental companionship and often not even for love. They had other women to turn to for that--the hetaerae, foreign women (not Athenian citizens) who were neither entitled to the protection nor subject to the restrictions of Athenian law.

> They were the only educated women in Athens. They studied all the arts, became acquainted with all new philosophical speculations, and interested themselves in politics. Women who thus cultivated their minds were sure to gain the esteem of the best men in Greece. Many of them also were women of high moral character, temperate, thoughtful, and earnest. . . . [11]

Free in body and free to possess a mind, they were persons as well as women, and it was with them that the great men of Athens discussed their pursuits and shared their most profound meditations. History has preserved the names of many of them: Leontium, Phryne, Lais, Diotima, and above all Aspasia, the brilliant and highly cultured woman whom Pericles divorced his legal wife to live with until his death, with such devotion that it was in all ways a marriage save in name.

With the death of Pericles, Athens passed on to a new period in its history. The absence of the menfolk during the Peloponnesian War had given women a taste of greater freedom, and by the end of the fifth century signs of unrest and of a questioning of traditional restrictions began to appear. The boldly independent women pictured by Aristophanes in his Lysistrata, Ecclesiazusae, and Thesmophoriazusae are no doubt broad comic exaggerations, but they must have been suggested by social changes of the time. Remarkable, too, are the women of Greek tragedy; they are "powerful agents of instruction, inspiration and propaganda," a far cry from the spiritless women we are used to hearing about.[12] Sophocles' Antigone, for example, embodies the perennial conflict between the edict of the state and the individual's conscience, the clash of public and private duty which is made real for us in the person of "a heroine of unflinching resolution and single concentration of purpose."[13] Euripides, more than any other, presented strong and vigorous women in his plays, as well as the injustice of their lot. His Medea, for example, cries out that

> of all things that have life and sense, we women are most wretched. For we are compelled to buy with gold a husband who is also--worst of all!--the master of our person. And on his character, good or bad, our whole fate depends.[14]

Greek women thus began to agitate for change, until by the time of Alexander the Great they had achieved at least partial emancipation. They participated actively in the cultural life of the time and contributed to the literature, science, philosophy, and art of Greece. Among them were

Agnodice, the doctor, and the philosophers Hipparchia, Melissa, Myia, Perictione, Phintys, and Theano. But by this time the democratic glories of Athens were gone, and the empire of Alexander had splintered into several monarchies and city-states. What brought about the decline? More than one author has gone so far as to agree with F. A. Wright that "the Greek world perished from one major cause, a low ideal of womanhood and a degradation of women which found expression both in literature and in social life"; these were "the canker-spots which, left unhealed, brought about the decay first of Athens and then of Greece."[15]

Such, then, was the state of women in Athens, but Athens was not all of Greece. To the north and west dwelt peoples whose women still retained privileges surviving from earlier times. None, though, went quite so far as Sparta. Spartan women came the closest to having real equality of any women in history. They could inherit and bequeath property, received the same physical training as men, even wrestled with them, and were not limited to one man but could indulge in free intercourse outside the bonds of marriage without the stigma of immorality. The goal in militaristic Sparta was to breed healthy children who would become good Spartan soldiers, and whatever actions served this end were permissible. As the men were often off at war, the women generally ran the estates and had a strong voice in government. Their freedom naturally excited the contempt of the Athenians, who mocked the Spartans for being ruled by their women. "Yes," replied Gorgo, the Spartan heroine, "but then we are the only ones who still bring men into the world."[16] Spartan women were proud, brave, and strong, certainly, but they were not free. Along with their men they were subjected to the rigid discipline and control of a state which manipulated their lives to its own ends. Some authors (in particular, Charles Seltman and L. J. Ludovici) have concluded that they were the freest, healthiest, and happiest women in history, a conclusion most difficult to defend. Spartan women may have been on a level of equality with their men, but it was the equality of slaves.

Martial spirit was by no means confined to Spartan women, though. One thinks immediately of the Amazons, the vigorous nation of warrior maidens said to have inhabited the mountains of Thrace and the Scythian north. Historians have long dismissed them as purely legendary, but the Amazons figure so prominently in ancient myth and tradition, in art and literature, and in the works of ancient historians that one begins to suspect that--like the stories of Troy and the palace of Knossos--they, too, had a basis in fact.

There can be no doubt, though, as to the historicity of their descendants--the warrior queens who ruled over several of the Hellenistic kingdoms, and who were not afraid, if need be, to declare war and to lead their troops personally into battle. Foremost among these were Artemisia, the queen of Caria, who conquered the Isle of Rhodes and built the Mausoleum, one of the Seven Wonders of the Ancient World; Dynamis, Queen of Bosporus; Euridyce, Queen of Macedonia; Laodice, Queen of Cappadocia and Bithynia; Cratesipolis, the Peloponnesian queen who commanded her own army of mercenaries; Tomyris, the Scythian queen who challenged the mighty Cyrus the Great in battle and slew him; and Teuta, the warrior queen who opposed Rome in the First Illyrian War.

Later ages produced worthy successors. Fulvia, Mark Antony's wife, to her husband's dismay stirred up a revolt against Octavian and caused the Perusine War. Other women fought valiantly against the encroachment of the Roman Empire; Zenobia, Queen of Palmyra, renounced allegiance to Rome and challenged Emperor Aurelian in battle. Cartimandua, on the other hand, queen of the Brigantes in northern Britain, collaborated with the Romans and successfully battled first her husband and then the neighboring tribes who resisted her. The greatest warrior queen of all, though, was undoubtedly Boadicea (or, more properly, Boudicca) of Britain. Outraged by the indignities heaped on herself and her daughters by the invading Romans, she declared war against them in 61 A.D., routed their legions, sacked the cities of London, Colchester, and St. Albans, and killed seventy thousand of the enemy before finally being defeated by the assembled might of Rome. Her speech to her troops, as recorded by Tacitus, is one of the noblest and most eloquent statements of resistance to tyranny ever written.[17]

By Boadicea's time Greece had lost its former strength, and a new power had taken its place: Rome. Its predecessors in Italy, the Etruscans, were notorious among the Greeks for the freedom of their women. Indeed,

> in a society where we see her mingling with such brilliance in the business and the pleasures of men, ... with an authority that was almost sovereign; artistic, cultivated, interested in hellenic refinements and the bringer of civilization to her home; finally venerated in the tomb as an emanation of divine power,

the Etruscan woman had so privileged a position that "it cannot be denied that Etruscan society in many respects has elements of both matriarchy and gynaecocracy."[18]

The conquering Romans, however, were firmly patriarchal. Whereas Etruscan women had their own individual first names, and Roman men were distinguished by three names, each one significant, the Roman woman was considered of so little individual worth that she had to settle for only one, the feminine form of her father's family name. Thus, Gaius Julius Caesar's daughter was called Julia, Marcus Tullius Cicero's, Tullia. In fact, so little ingenuity was expended on names for girls that sisters regularly shared the same one, distinguished only as "the elder" and "the younger," or Martia Secunda, for example, and Martia Tertia--Martia the second, Martia the third, and so forth. Only late in the Empire did this practice change.

From the earliest times, women in the patriarchal society of Rome were seen as perpetual minors under the law. They were first under the guardianship of their fathers, or nearest male relatives, until marriage, when they passed to the authority of their husbands. Legally more enslaved than Greek women, they could not act as witnesses, sign wills, make contracts, or inherit property. Such was their legal position, but before long it had ceased to correspond to the reality of the Roman matron's social position. In practice she was an integral part of Roman society. In the home she was absolute mistress, the *domina*; she was not hidden away in the women's quarters, but sat in the central room of the house, from which she supervised the work of the slaves and the education of the children. She received her husband's guests and even dined with them (a custom which shocked the Greeks), and she was free to leave the house to attend the theatre, the public games, or the baths. On the street men gave her the right of way, and even consuls made room for her to pass. She shared in the business of her husband and was often consulted by him on affairs of state, and, through various legal evasions until the law was finally changed, she often owned and managed her own property. Clearly,

> with her marriage to a citizen of Rome a Roman woman reached a position never attained by the women of any other nation in the ancient world. Nowhere else were women held in such high respect; nowhere else did they exert so strong and beneficent an influence.[19]

Roman women were determined and spirited ladies and, by exerting constant pressure for reform, they gradually became emancipated from the fetters of ancient law and custom. Their legal status was brought into line with their social importance, until "their actual position became far better than it has ever been since, until very recent times."[20] When in 195 B.C. the Oppian Law was up for repeal (a stringent law which forbade women to wear jewelry or expensive clothes, or to ride in carriages in the city), the women responded to those who wanted the law retained with tactics much like those of the modern suffragettes. They canvassed for votes, surrounded the houses of their leading opponents, marched on the Senate, and demonstrated in the streets. Understandably enough, the law was repealed. Cato the Elder, an old traditionalist, was so provoked at this that he grumbled,

> If every married man had been concerned to ensure that his own wife looked up to him and respected his rightful position as her husband, we should not have half this trouble with women _en masse_. Instead, women have become so powerful that our independence has been lost in our own homes and is now being trampled and stamped underfoot in public. We have failed to restrain them as individuals, and now they have combined to reduce us to our present panic.[21]

These women were not a force to be trifled with. Roman history affords us numerous examples of exceptional power, talent, and character on the part of Roman matrons, a record all the more remarkable when compared to that of their Greek counterparts. First and foremost was Cornelia, the mother of the Gracchi and symbol of matronly virtue, who refused the hand of a king to educate her children for their pivotal role in the politics of the Republic; besides her political influence, she was herself an author, a scholar, and a friend of scholars. Two fragments of letters attributed to her survive which, together with six elegies by the poetess Sulpicia and a satire by a different Sulpicia, form the entire extant corpus of Roman women's writings.

Livia, the first Roman empress, was also a symbol of matronly virtue; she was highly esteemed by her husband Augustus, whom she influenced greatly with her intelligent advice, and after his death she continued to exercise a moderating restraint on the excesses of his successor. And there were many other noble matrons: Pompey's wife Cornelia, Agrippina the Elder, Arria, Plotina, Sabina, Antonia, and Octavia, Augustus's self-sacrificing sister and wife of Mark Antony, whose humanity and generosity in raising her husband's children (by herself, by his first wife Fulvia, and by Cleopatra) earned her the love of the Roman people.

If the Roman woman was free to exercise her mind and her virtues, she was likewise free to abandon herself to vice. The pages of the historians are "sprinkled with the most lurid accounts of feminine debauchery."[22] Augustus's own daughter and granddaughter, Julia Major and Minor, were banished for adultery, and Messalina, wife of the emperor Claudius, would sneak out of the palace at night and head for the brothels, there to take on all comers. After her death Claudius married Agrippina the Younger, an ambitious woman "who yielded to no one in depravity" and who was, "appropriately enough, the mother of Nero."[23] In later years she wrote her memoirs, the loss of which historians have mourned for the light they could have thrown on the politics of the early Empire. And there were many others: Clodia, Poppaea, Faustina, Sempronia, Locusta (whose specialty was poisoning people), and the matrons who went so far as to register themselves as prostitutes in order to avoid prosecution for adultery.

The problem, at least in part, was that the Roman woman, while achieving social and legal emancipation such as has scarcely been equalled since, failed to obtain any political responsibilities to go with it. Her dilemma has been best expounded by Simone de Beauvoir:

> The fact is that the matrons made no very good use of their new liberty; but it is also true that they were not allowed to turn it to positive account.... When the collapse of the family made the ancient virtues of private life useless and outdated, there was no longer any established morality for woman, since public life and its virtues remained inaccessible to her.... The Roman woman of the old Republic had a place on earth, but she was chained to it for lack of abstract rights and economic independence; the Roman woman of the decline was the typical product of false emancipation, having only an empty liberty in a world of which man remained in fact the sole master: she was free--but for nothing.[24]

But, even as the Roman woman's status was at its height, the dark forces of change were gathering to undermine it. A new religion, with a far different ideal of womanhood, had taken hold in the Empire. "The conversion of the Roman world to Christianity," says one authority, "was to bring a great change in woman's status."[25] Indeed so, for the advances made by women under paganism were soon lost under the conquering banner of Judaeo-Christian patriarchy, as interpreted by the misogynist St. Paul.

The old ways lingered on, though, for many years.

One of the final outposts of pagan culture, and the last repository of the wisdom of the ancients, was the great library at Alexandria and the community of scholars there assembled. Foremost among these was Hypatia, leader of the Neoplatonic school of philosophy and the last representative of the Greek tradition of free creative inquiry. Unquestionably the greatest woman philosopher who has ever lived, she taught publicly and had a large number of disciples, who were attracted by her immense learning and eloquence, her great beauty and modesty, and the maturity of her wisdom. She was in addition a logician and a mathematician, whose "learned comments have elucidated the geometry of Apollonius and Diophantus; ... persons most illustrious for their rank or merit were impatient to visit the female philosopher."[26]

To many zealous Christians of the time, who feared a resurgence of paganism, such gatherings were suspect. Time had run out for the pagan intellectuals, especially for the young woman who audaciously presumed to teach men and who was thus persecuted not only for her religion but "on account of her knowledge which overstepped all bounds" for a woman.[27] In 415 A.D. she met her death at the hands of a sectarian Christian mob, whose deed Gibbon describes as follows:

> On a fatal day, in the holy season of Lent, Hypatia was torn from her chariot, stripped naked, dragged to the church, and inhumanly butchered by ... a troop of savage and merciless fanatics: her flesh was scraped from her bones with sharp oyster-shells, and her quivering limbs were delivered to the flames.[28]

Her writings, along with the rest of the Alexandrian Library, met a similar fate. Classical civilization, long in the throes of death, had gasped its last.

In reviewing the chronicle of woman's history in the ancient world, it is a tantalizing circumstance that the first individual it reveals was the greatest woman poet, and the last, the greatest philosopher. Between them ranges a broad spectrum of women--some of whom realized the full nobility of humanity, some the full degeneracy of it, and most, only its mediocrity. If they were no better than their men, neither were they any worse, but such has always been the case. And so, no doubt, will it always be.

Notes

1. Sir Henry Maine, Rede Lecture for 1875, cited by John Addington Symonds, *Studies of the Greek Poets*, II (New York: Harper & Brothers, [n. d.]), pp. 420-421.

2. Herodotus, *History*, i, 173.

3. Jacques Heurgon, *Daily Life of the Etruscans*, trans. James Kirkup (New York: Macmillan Co., 1964), p. 86.

4. Elizabeth Gould Davis, *The First Sex* (Baltimore: Penguin Books, 1971), p. 40.

5. Page Smith, *Daughters of the Promised Land* (Boston: Little, Brown and Co., 1970), p. 9.

6. R. W. Macan, "Herodotus and Thucydides," *The Cambridge Ancient History*, ed. J. B. Bury, S. A. Cook, and F. E. Adcock, V (New York: Macmillan, 1927), p. 407.

7. Thucydides, *The Peloponnesian War*, ii. 45.

8. James Donaldson, *Woman: Her Position and Influence in Ancient Greece and Rome, and Among the Early Christians* (London: Longmans, Green, and Co., 1907), p. 55.

9. C. M. Bowra, *Greek Poetry from Alcman to Simonides* (2nd ed., rev.; Oxford: Clarendon Press, 1961), p. 240.

10. Xenophon, Oeconomica, vii. 5, cited by Robert Flacelière, Daily Life in Greece at the Time of Pericles, trans. Peter Green (New York: Macmillan, 1965), p. 56.

11. Donaldson, op. cit., p. 58.

12. Sherman Plato Young, The Women of Greek Drama (New York: Exposition Press, 1953), p. 174.

13. Ibid., p. 64.

14. Euripides, Medea, 230-236, cited by John Langdon-Davies, A Short History of Women (New York: Viking, 1927), p. 173.

15. F. A. Wright, Feminism in Greek Literature from Homer to Aristotle (London: Routledge, 1923), p. 1.

16. Plutarch, Life of Lycurgus, xiv. 47, cited by Verena Zinserling, Women in Greece and Rome, trans. L. A. Jones (New York: Abner Schram, 1973), p. 33.

17. Tacitus, Annals, xiv. 35.

18. Heurgon, op. cit., pp. 96 and 85.

19. Mary Johnston, Roman Life (Glenview, Ill.: Scott, Foresman and Co., 1957), p. 137.

20. John Langdon-Davies, A Short History of Women (New York: Viking, 1927), p. 176.

21. Livy, History of Rome, xxxiv. 2, cited by J. P. V. D. Balsdon, Roman Women: Their History and Habits (London: Bodley Head, 1962), pp. 33-34.

22. Smith, op. cit., p. 12.

23. Ibid., pp. 12-13.

24. Simone de Beauvoir, The Second Sex, trans. H. M. Parshley (New York: Bantam Books, 1970), pp. 88-89.

25. J. P. V. D. Balsdon, Roman Women: Their History and Habits (London: Bodley Head, 1962), p. 283.

26. Edward Gibbon, The Decline and Fall of the Roman Empire, II (New York: The Modern Library, [1954]), p. 816.

27. Hesychius, Meursii Opera, vii, cited by Gibbon, p. 816, n. 25. The translation is my own.

28. Gibbon, loc. cit.

BIBLIOGRAPHY

Balsdon, John Percy Vyvian Dacre. Roman Women: Their History and Habits. London: Bodley Head, 1962.

Beauvoir, Simone de. The Second Sex, trans. H. M. Parshley. New York: Bantam Books, 1970.

Bell, Susan G. (ed.). Women: From the Greeks to the French Revolution. Belmont, Calif.: Wadsworth Publishing Co., 1973.

Bowra, C. M. Greek Lyric Poetry from Alcman to Simonides. 2nd ed., rev. Oxford: The Clarendon Press, 1961.

Bury, J. B., S. A. Cook, and F. E. Adcock (eds.). The Cambridge Ancient History. Vol. V, Athens, 478-401 B.C. New York: The Macmillan Co., 1927.

Davis, Elizabeth Gould. The First Sex. Baltimore: Penguin Books, 1971.

Diner, Helen. Mothers and Amazons: The First Feminine History of Culture, trans. John Philip Lundin. New York: Julian Press, 1965.

Donaldson, James. Woman: Her Position and Influence in Ancient Greece and Rome, and Among the Early Christians. London: Longmans, Green, and Co., 1907.

Flacelière, Robert. Daily Life in Greece at the Time of Pericles, trans. Peter Green. New York: The Macmillan Co., 1965.

Gibbon, Edward. The Decline and Fall of the Roman Empire. 3 vols. New York: The Modern Library, [1954].

Heurgon, Jacques. Daily Life of the Etruscans, trans. James Kirkup. New York: The Macmillan Co., 1964.

Johnston, Mary. Roman Life. Glenview, Ill.: Scott, Foresman and Co., 1957.

Langdon-Davies, John. A Short History of Women. New York: The Viking Press, 1927.

Ludovici, L. J. The Final Inequality. New York: Tower Publications, 1972.

Macurdy, Grace Harriet. Hellenistic Queens: A Study of Woman-Power in Macedonia, Seleucid Syria, and Ptolemaic Egypt. Johns Hopkins University Studies in Archaeology, No. 14. Baltimore: Johns Hopkins University Press, 1932.

_______. Vassal-Queens and Some Contemporary Women in the Roman Empire. Johns Hopkins University Studies in Archaeology, No. 22. Baltimore: Johns Hopkins University Press, 1937.

Seltman, Charles. Women in Antiquity. New York: St. Martin's Press, [1956].

Slater, Philip E. The Glory of Hera: Greek Mythology and the Greek Family. Boston: Beacon Press, 1968.

Smith, Page. Daughters of the Promised Land: Women in American History. Boston: Little, Brown and Co., 1970.

Symonds, John Addington. Studies of the Greek Poets. 2 vols. New York: Harper & Brothers, [n.d.].

Thucydides. The Peloponnesian War, trans. Richard Crawley. New York: The Modern Library, 1951.

Wright, Frederick Adam. Feminism in Greek Literature from Homer to Aristotle. London: George Routledge & Sons, 1923.

Young, Sherman Plato. The Women of Greek Drama. New York: Exposition Press, 1953.

Zinserling, Verena. Women in Greece and Rome, trans. L. A. Jones. New York: Abner Schram, 1973.

II

FORMAT AND PROCEDURES

Even a brief look at women in antiquity reveals a rich and fascinating history, worthy of serious, scholarly study. Most such study, however, remains undone, and much of what does exist was written in the nineteenth century or the first two decades of the twentieth--though often with a quite modern feminist slant. The recent revival of interest has already given rise to new publications and college courses, and may be expected to so continue. Women's studies have come into their own in the last few years, but most work has been done on current problems or, at best, the history of woman since the sixteenth century. The study of women in classical antiquity has long been a neglected field; little research and even less bibliographic effort has been devoted to it.

In fact, only one survey of the literature exists: a bibliographic essay by Sarah B. Pomeroy, "Selected Bibliography on Women in Antiquity," in the special "Women in Antiquity" issue of *Arethusa* (VI, Spring, 1973, 125-157). An excellent general introduction to the material on women in Greece and Rome, early Christianity, and ancient matriarchy, Ms. Pomeroy's work is distinguished by its perceptive commentary and assured familiarity with the subject, particularly with the major scholarly controversies; she includes, also, a suggested outline and reading list for an undergraduate course on women in antiquity. However, it is a highly selective work, and the citations are limited by and large to fairly recent publications. A large number of valuable works, especially older ones, are omitted, and older works (as already observed) constitute a major source of study on the subject. Specialized investigations--in particular, studies of individual women--are left out completely in Ms. Pomeroy's short survey, but such works are essential for serious, detailed study. Finally, a major impediment to her essay's use is its narrow intended audience: "designed primarily for use by classicists intending to introduce undergraduate courses on women in antiquity," and published in an obscure classical journal with a very small circulation. Hence, both the interested student and the scholarly researcher who wish to find out more about ancient women soon discover that there is really no one comprehensive guide to turn to for help in locating material. This lack is a big obstacle to future research, and a bibliography such as this is sorely needed to help fill the gap.

I have therefore compiled this bibliography of materials about the historical women of antiquity, specifically ancient Greece and Rome, from the earliest records to 476 A.D. It also covers women among the Minoans, Etruscans, the Hellenistic kingdoms, and some provinces of the Roman Empire. Material on women in Africa or the Near East has not normally been included. Since one can hardly learn about women in general without learning about specific women, biographies of individuals are included and make up a goodly portion of the works listed. Cleopatra, however, has arbitrarily been excluded; the literature about her is so voluminous as to require a bibliography all its own. For the same reason, only a selective list of books and articles on

Sappho is given, and all works of purely literary or textual criticism are omitted as outside the scope of this book. Those interested in these women will find the following bibliographies helpful:

On Cleopatra--Theodore Besterman's eight-page Bibliography of Cleopatra (London: [n. n.], 1926), which contains 189 items; for newer material, the annotated bibliography on pages 220-231 of Hans Volkmann's Cleopatra: A Study in Politics and Propaganda, trans. T. J. Cadoux (New York: Sagamore Press, 1958); and most recently, Michael Grant's selective bibliography on pages 239-247 of his Cleopatra (London: Weidenfeld and Nicolson, 1972).

On Sappho--For older materials see Antonio Cipollini's Saffo: Parte I, Studio Critico-Bibliografico (Milano: Fratelli Dumolard, 1890); also, the editions of Sappho's works by Edwin Marion Cox (London: Williams and Norgate, 1925) and Henry Thornton Wharton (New York: Brentano's, 1920; actually, though, the 1896 revision is most recent, as the 1920 version merely reprints the original 1885 edition). More recent materials may be located through the annual bibliography of classical studies, L'Année Philologique.

Listings for all other women are as complete as possible, including (since they are scarce and hard to find) works of literary, but not textual, criticism on the writings of the lesser-known women poets. Christian saints are omitted, as information on them is available from other sources.

Intended as a guide to the political, social, legal, and literary achievements and treatment of women in antiquity, this bibliography includes original classical sources as well as modern studies of the topic. However, this is not a concordance to every little mention of a woman by any classical author, so only those ancient works primarily involved with the subject have been chosen for inclusion. They are listed both in the original language and in a few representative English translations, or in dual-language editions.

Modern works (published since 1872) have been included both in English and in foreign tongues. The list of modern works attempts to be a comprehensive guide to the material written on this topic in the English language, with selective coverage of items in foreign languages, as well. Non-English materials are limited to the following languages: Greek, Latin, French, German, and Italian. Only print items--books and journal articles of a factual nature--are listed. Fictionalized accounts or modern dramatic works about ancient women are outside the scope of this paper.

The material collected here is intended for use in an academic library. It can serve as an introduction to the literature for college undergraduates in either women's studies or ancient history classes, or as a starting point for more advanced research by graduate students and professors. As a knowledge of the original sources from which our information is derived is vital for serious study, classical works of importance in the field are included. In order to make the bibliography of greater use to students and researchers, all relevant works I have been able to discover bibliographically have been listed, although only those I have actually been able to examine are annotated. Also, because many works not devoted exclusively to women in antiquity contain excellent chapters on the subject, several books about Greek or Roman culture, or about women's history in general, have been included.

A thorough search of the literature has failed to turn up any works which serve a similar purpose, excepting of course the bibliographic essay by Ms. Pomeroy, which has already been discussed. Otherwise, some books on the subject do have useful bibliographies at the end; most notable are James Donaldson's Woman: Her Position and Influence in Ancient Greece and Rome, and Among the Early Christians, 1907 (for older works), and more recently, Verena Zinserling's Women in Greece and Rome, 1973. Neither of these is annotated. To be sure, many fine bibliographies about women in general have been produced, but none give more than superficial treatment for women in antiquity. Particularly noteworthy among such works are Lucinda Cisler's Women: A Bibliography (privately printed, Box 240, New York City, 10024); Female Studies I-IV, the collection of college syllabi and reading lists put together by the Modern Language Association's Commission on the Status of Women and published by KNOW, Inc. (Box 86031, Pittsburgh, Pa. 15221); Norma Ireland's Index to Women of the World from Ancient to Modern Times (Westwood, Mass.: Faxon, 1970); the Scarecrow Press book, Womanhood Media, by Helen Wheeler, 1972; and Women Studies Abstracts (Box 1, Rush, N.Y. 14543), begun in 1972.

As there is no major bibliographic source for its topic, this list was built up by gathering citations from many sources. In addition to the works listed above, reference sources in the classics and in history, bibliographies at the ends of books, and even footnotes supplied many titles. Such general aids as the National Union Catalog, the General Catalogue of the British Museum, Books in Print, and the Cumulative Book Index were searched, as were major periodical indexes. Of great value were the annual issues of the International Bibliography of Historical Sciences and L'Année Philologique. These tools were scanned, both under general subject headings (such as "Women in Greece") and under the individual names of important women of antiquity.

In order to annotate the items thus located, several libraries in California were searched. Besides the San Jose State University Library, I have drawn upon the collections of the University of California at Berkeley, the Orradre Library of the University of Santa Clara, the San Jose Public Library, Santa Clara Public Library, the Santa Clara County system, and the county libraries of Santa Cruz and San Benito Counties.

Many works were examined which proved of no help for this bibliography. The following sources, however, were the most valuable in finding titles:

Aldous, Joan, and Reuben Hill. International Bibliography of Research in Marriage and the Family, 1900-1964. [Minneapolis]: University of Minnesota Press, 1967.

The American Historical Association. Guide to Historical Literature. New York: The Macmillan Co., 1961.

L'Année Philologique de l'Antiquité Gréco-Latine, ed. J. Marouzeau et al. Vols. I-IV, XVI-XXV, XXVIII-XLII. Paris: Société d'Édition "Les Belles Lettres," 1928-30, 1946-55, 1958-73.

Balsdon, J. P. V. D. Roman Women: Their History and Habits. London: Bodley Head, 1962.

Besterman, Theodore. A World Bibliography of Bibliographies. 5 vols. 4th ed. Lausanne: Societas Bibliographica, 1965.

Bibliographic Index: A Cumulative Bibliography of Bibliographies, 1937-April, 1974. New York: The H. W. Wilson Co., 1945-74.

Biography Index, January, 1946-May, 1974. New York: The H. W. Wilson Co., 1949-74.

Boak, Arthur, and Wm. Sinnigen. A History of Rome to A. D. 565. 5th ed. New York: The Macmillan Co., 1965.

Book Review Digest, 1905-June, 1974. New York: The H. W. Wilson Co., 1905-74.

Books in Print, 1973. 2 vols. New York: R. R. Bowker Co., 1973.

Botsford, G. W., and E. G. Sihler (eds.). *Hellenic Civilization*. New York: Columbia University Press, 1929.

Briffault, Robert. *The Mothers: A Study of the Origins of Sentiments and Institutions, Vol. III*. New York: The Macmillan Co., 1927.

British Humanities Index, 1962-January to March, 1974. London: The Library Association, 1963-74.

British Museum. Department of Printed Books. *General Catalogue of Printed Books, to 1955*. 263 vols. London: The Trustees of the British Museum, 1959-66.

________. *General Catalogue of Printed Books. Ten-Year Supplement, 1956-1965*. 50 vols. London: The Trustees of the British Museum, 1968.

________. *General Catalogue of Printed Books. Five-Year Supplement, 1966-1970*. 26 vols. London: The Trustees of the British Museum, 1971-72.

British Museum. *Subject Index of the Modern Works Added to the Library of the British Museum in the Years 1881-1945*. London: The Trustees of the British Museum, 1902-53.

California. San Jose State University. Library. Card Catalog.

California. University, Berkeley. Library. *Author-Title Catalog*. 115 vols. Boston: G. K. Hall & Co., 1963.

California. University. Institute of Library Research. *University of California Union Catalog of Monographs Cataloged by the Nine Campuses from 1963 through 1967*. 47 vols. Berkeley: Institute of Library Research, University of California, 1972.

California. University, Los Angeles. *Dictionary Catalog of the University Library, 1919-1962*. 129 vols. Boston: G. K. Hall & Co., 1963.

The Cambridge Ancient History. Vols. IV-XII. New York: The Macmillan Co., 1926-39.

Cervantes, Lucius F. "Woman's Changing Role in Society," *Thought*, XL (Autumn, 1965), 325-368.

Chambers's Encyclopaedia. 15 vols. Rev. ed. London: International Learning Systems Corp., 1973.

Cisler, Lucinda. *Women: A Bibliography*. 6th ed. New York: By the Author, 1970.

Cumulative Book Index, 1928-May, 1974. New York: The H. W. Wilson Co., 1933-74.

Daremberg, Charles, and Edmond Saglio (eds.). *Dictionnaire des Antiquités Grecques et Romaines*. 6 vols. Graz, Austria: Akademische Druck- u. Verlagsanstalt, 1963.

Donaldson, James. *Woman: Her Position and Influence in Ancient Greece and Rome, and Among the Early Christians*. London: Longmans, Green, and Co., 1907.

Enciclopedia Italiana di Scienze, Lettere ed Arti. 35 vols. 1949 ed. Roma: Istituto della Enciclopedia Italiana, 1950.

Encyclopaedia Britannica. 24 vols. 1971 ed. Chicago: Encyclopaedia Britannica, Inc., 1972.

Encyclopedia Americana. 30 vols. New York: Americana Corp., 1974.

Essay and General Literature Index, 1900-June, 1974. New York: The H. W. Wilson Co., 1934-74.

Gerber, Douglas E. "A Survey of Publications on Greek Lyric Poetry Since 1952, II," *Classical World*, LXI (April, 1968), 317-330.

A Guide to Historical Literature, ed. William Henry Allison et al. New York: The Macmillan Co., 1931.

Gwinup, Thomas, and Fidelia Dickinson. *Greek and Roman Authors: A Checklist of Criticism*. Metuchen, N.J.: Scarecrow Press, 1973.

Hoffsten, Ruth Bertha. Roman Women of Rank of the Early Empire in Public Life as Portrayed by Dio, Paterculus, Suetonius, and Tacitus. Philadelphia: University of Pennsylvania, 1939.

Howe, Florence, and Carol Ahlum (eds.). Female Studies, II and III. Pittsburgh: KNOW, Inc., 1970-71.

Index to Religious Periodical Literature, 1949-July-December, 1973. [Chicago]: American Theological Library Association, 1953-74.

International Bibliography of Historical Sciences. Vols. I-XXXVIII. Paris: Librairie Armand Colin, 1930-71.

International Index to Periodicals, 1907-March, 1965. New York: The H. W. Wilson Co., 1907-65.

Ireland, Norma Olin. Index to Women of the World from Ancient to Modern Times. Westwood, Mass.: F. W. Faxon Co., 1970.

Kellaway, William. Bibliography of Historical Works Issued in the United Kingdom, 1961-1965. London: University of London Institute of Historical Research, 1967.

Kirkwood, G. M. "A Survey of Recent Publications Concerning Classical Greek Lyric Poetry," Classical Weekly, XLVII (November 30, 1953), 33-42.

Lewis, Naphtali, and Meyer Reinhold. Roman Civilization. 2 vols. New York: Harper & Row, 1966.

Logasa, Hannah. Historical Non-Fiction. 8th ed. Brooklawn, N.J.: McKinley Publishing Co., 1964.

London. University. Warburg Institute. Library. Catalog of the Warburg Institute Library. 2 vols. Boston: G. K. Hall & Co., 1961.

Macurdy, Grace Harriet. Hellenistic Queens: A Study of Woman-Power in Macedonia, Seleucid Syria, and Ptolemaic Egypt. Johns Hopkins University Studies in Archaeology, No. 14. Baltimore: Johns Hopkins University Press, 1932.

_______. Vassal-Queens and Some Contemporary Women in

the Roman Empire. Johns Hopkins University Studies in Archaeology, No. 22. Baltimore: Johns Hopkins University Press, 1937.

Nairn, John A. Classical Hand-List. 3rd ed. Oxford: B. H. Blackwell, 1960.

The New Encyclopaedia Britannica. 30 vols. 15th ed. Chicago: Encyclopaedia Britannica, Inc., 1974.

Nineteenth Century Readers' Guide to Periodical Literature, 1890-1899, with Supplementary Indexing, 1900-1922. 2 vols. New York: The H. W. Wilson Co., 1944.

The Oxford Classical Dictionary, ed. N. G. L. Hammond and H. H. Scullard. 2nd ed. Oxford: The Clarendon Press, 1970.

Paris. Bibliothèque Nationale. Catalogue Général des Livres Imprimés de la Bibliothèque Nationale: Auteurs. 197 vols. Paris: Imprimerie Nationale, 1897-in progress.

Pauly, August Friedrich von. Pauly's Real-Encyclopädie der Classischen Altertumswissenschaft, ed. Georg Wissowa. Stuttgart: Alfred Druckenmüller Verlag, 1892-in progress.

Pomeroy, Sarah B. "Selected Bibliography on Women in Antiquity," Arethusa, VI (Spring, 1973), 125-157.

Public Library Catalog, ed. Estelle A. Fidell. 5th ed. New York: The H. W. Wilson Co., 1969.

Readers' Guide to Periodical Literature, 1900-June 10, 1974. New York: The H. W. Wilson Co., 1905-74.

Sandys, John Edwin (ed.). A Companion to Latin Studies. 3rd ed. New York: Hafner Publishing Co., 1963.

Social Sciences and Humanities Index, April, 1965-March, 1974. New York: The H. W. Wilson Co., 1966-74.

Stern, Bernhard J. "Woman, Position in Society: Historical," Encyclopaedia of the Social Sciences, 1948, XV, 450-51.

Subject Guide to Books in Print, 1973. 2 vols. New York: R. R. Bowker Co., 1973.

Thompson, Lawrence S. A Bibliography of American Doctoral Dissertations in Classical Studies and Related Fields. Hamden, Conn.: Shoe String Press, 1968.

Tobias, Sheila (ed.). Female Studies, I: A Collection of College Syllabi and Reading Lists. Pittsburgh: KNOW, Inc., 1970.

The United States Catalog: Books in Print January 1, 1928. 4th ed. New York: The H. W. Wilson Co., 1928.

U.S. Library of Congress. Library of Congress Catalog; Books: Subjects, 1950-July-September, 1973. Washington: The Library of Congress, 1955-73.

Voigt, Melvin J., and Joseph H. Treyz (eds.). Books for College Libraries. Chicago: American Library Association, 1967.

Wheeler, Helen. Womanhood Media: Current Resources About Women. Metuchen, N.J.: Scarecrow Press, 1972.

Whibley, Leonard (ed.). A Companion to Greek Studies. 4th ed. Cambridge: The University Press, 1931.

Women Studies Abstracts. Vols. I-III, no. 1. Rush, N.Y.: Women Studies Abstracts, 1972-74.

Zinserling, Verena. Women in Greece and Rome, trans. L. A. Jones. New York: Abner Schram, 1973.

All items in this bibliography are listed in Part III, both annotated and unannotated items together. Ancient sources are given first, then modern works. Listed first are the writings of ancient women themselves, followed by the relevant works of other (male) authors of antiquity. The modern works are organized in a simple subject arrangement: general works on both Greece and Rome first, followed by works solely on Greek women, then by works dealing with Rome. All items within each subdivision are arranged alphabetically by author, then by title. To the left of the items, in the margin, unique identifying numbers are assigned consecutively from beginning to end, to serve as finding aids when using the indexes, which follow the bibliography.

Preceding the indexes is a key to the abbreviations used in them. There are two indexes. The first, a unique and distinguishing feature of this bibliography, lists by name many important women of antiquity, followed by the dates of their lives and a brief summary of who they were; identification numbers referring to the items listed in the bibliography follow this information. Thus, the user who wants specific works about, say, Praxilla can find them simply by turning to her name in this index. A few proper names referring to more than one individual (such as Amazons, Sibyls, and Vestal Virgins) are also included here. The authorities used to establish the names and dates in this index are:

The Oxford Classical Dictionary, ed. N. G. L. Hammond and H. H. Scullard. 2nd ed. Oxford: Clarendon Press, 1970;

Norma Ireland's Index to Women of the World from Ancient to Modern Times. Westwood, Mass.: F. W. Faxon Co., 1970;

The Encyclopaedia Britannica, 1974 edition; and,

William Smith (ed.). Dictionary of Greek and Roman Biography and Mythology. 3 vols. Boston: Little, Brown, & Co., 1890.

The second index lists all the authors, editors, and translators listed in the bibliography, followed by the identifying numbers of their works. Ancient women with extant writings are thus listed in both this and the first index.

The indexes are arranged alphabetically, word by word, and all diacritical marks, such as umlauts, are disregarded in determining this order. Names beginning with "Mc" (such as McCabe) are filed as if spelled "Mac."

The whole subject matter of women in antiquity is rich in possibilities. This bibliography is only a start, and further work still needs to be done. Comprehensive, up-to-date, and annotated bibliographies are wanting for Sappho, Cleopatra, women in Egypt, women in the Near East, and ancient women as interpreted in modern fiction and drama. A bibliographic guide to the large body of material about goddesses and the position of women in ancient mythology and religion sorely needs doing, also. Finally, the student interested in further information about any of the women listed here, and many others besides, will find articles in the following works most helpful:

The Oxford Classical Dictionary (see above);

August Friedrich von Pauly. Pauly's Real-Encyclopädie der Classischen Altertumswissenschaft, ed. Georg Wissowa. Stuttgart: Alfred Druckenmüller Verlag, 1892-in progress (generally cited as Pauly-Wissowa); and,

William Smith (ed.). Dictionary of Greek and Roman Biography and Mythology (see above).

For too long this topic has been curiously neglected, by both scholars and the general public. Few people, if asked to name five women of antiquity, could probably go beyond Cleopatra and Sappho. In these days when women are consciously examining their lot and trying to establish their own history and heritage, it seems that the full story of women in the ancient past, during a most important era in human history, has yet to be told. It is hoped that this bibliography may help make that story easier to tell.

III

BIBLIOGRAPHY ON WOMEN IN ANTIQUITY

ANCIENT SOURCES

Women Authors--Works by and about Them

SAPPHO

1. Bascoul, J. M. F. _Ἡ ἁγνὰ Σαπφώ: La Chaste Sappho de Lesbos et le Mouvement Féministe à Athènes au IVe Siècle avant J.-C._ Paris: Librairie Universitaire, 1911.

   This monograph begins with a discussion of Sappho's most famous poem, and of later parodies and paraphrases of it; a photograph of the poem in manuscript is included. The early Aeolian and Dorian woman, the author goes on to say, had great freedom, in contrast to the Athenians. The author's thesis is that a feminist movement was afoot in Athens during the fourth century B.C., and the parodies of Sappho are part of the reaction men made to this movement, an effort to lessen the stature of this liberated woman. It was then, also, that Sappho's reputation was blackened with charges of perversion (centuries after her death), and the word "lesbian" received its present connotation.

2. ________. _La Chaste Sappho de Lesbos et Stesichore, dont la Concurrence et les Prétentions lui Inspirèrent l'Ode II: Les Trois Dernières Strophes, Manquant à ce Poème Sont Reconstituées Ici, pour la Première Fois, au Moyen de Deux Fragments dont Voici le Plus Mutilé ... Les Prétendues Amies de Sappho._ Paris: H. Welter, 1913.

3. Bowra, C. M. _Greek Lyric Poetry from Alcman to Simonides._ 2d ed., rev. Oxford: The Clarendon Press, 1961.

   Chapter V, pages 176-240, is an excellent critical interpretation of Sappho's poetry: her technique, principle subjects, and what we can learn from it about her life. Bowra concentrates especially on the emotional power of her work, its passionate directness, her assurance and consciousness of self, and her main inspirations--love and the cult of beauty. The poems are quoted in Greek with English translation.

4. Cipollini, Antonio. *Saffo: Parte I, Studio Critico-Bibliografico; Parte II, La Gloria di Saffo.* Milano: Fratelli Dumolard, 1890.

Although quite old now, this work is still valuable for its bibliography of some five hundred items.

5. Green, Peter. "In Search of Sappho," *Horizon,* VIII (Spring, 1966), 105-111.

Green, while doing research for a novel about her, went to Sappho's home, the island of Lesbos, to better understand her. He has written here a substantial introduction, and one of the most enjoyable, in which he reviews her history and that of her poems, and ends by accepting all the legends about her: her homosexuality and her suicide jump.

6. Heintze, Helga von. *Das Bildnis der Sappho.* Mainz: Kupferberg, 1966.

7. Lobel, Edgar, and Denys Page (eds.). *Poetarum Lesbiorum Fragmenta.* Oxford: Clarendon Press, 1955.

This edition of the surviving fragments of the poets of Lesbos, notably Sappho, also contains the works of Alcaeus and fragments of unknown authorship. "Lobel and Page" is very conservative regarding even obvious emendations, allowing few conjectural readings, and is universally considered by scholars as the most complete, authoritative edition of Sappho's poems. The text of her fragments is on pages 1-110, and a full index of all her words is given at the back.

8. Mackail, John William. *Lectures on Greek Poetry.* London: Longmans, Green & Co., 1926.

"The Age of Freedom: Sappho," pages 83-112, is an eloquent essay on Sappho, attempting to convey the essence of her poetry and her place in Greek literature.

9. Mora, Édith. *Sappho, Histoire d'un Poète et Traduction Intégrale de l'Oeuvre.* Paris: Flammarion, 1966.

Ms. Mora aims to give the intelligent, Greekless

French reader an understanding of the "real" Sappho behind the legends--her life, her work, and her reputation. She investigates the myths surrounding her life and death, discusses the manuscript sources for the poems, and analyzes Sappho's poetic technique. Also she includes a French translation of all her poems, an extensive bibliography, and a list of the original manuscripts.

10. Page, Denys Lionel. Sappho and Alcaeus: An Introduction to the Study of Ancient Lesbian Poetry. Oxford: Clarendon Press, 1955.

This is one of the most important, recent critical works on the Lesbian poets. The first half of the book is devoted to Sappho and is divided into two sections. The first presents twelve of her longer poems, practically all of which any coherent idea can be gained. Each poem is treated individually; first the text is set out, then a translation, technical commentary on individual words, etc., followed by a more general interpretation. The second section assesses "The Contents and Character of Sappho's Poetry" in general, concentrating on the Epithalamia, the prominence of Aphrodite, and Sappho's moral character.

11. Prentice, William K. "Sappho," Classical Philology, XIII (October, 1918), 347-360.

A well-written and scholarly article, this reviews what is known about Sappho, refuting the charges against Sappho's moral character. Prentice asserts that she felt for her girls only a natural, impulsive, "untainted affection for a friend," which we are unable to appreciate in these decadent times.

12. Robinson, David M. Sappho and Her Influence. (Our Debt to Greece and Rome.) New York: Cooper Square Publishers, 1963.

One of the most extensive reviews of the influence of Sappho in later ages, this book gives a summary of her life and work, and then discusses her influence on art and music, and on the literatures of Greece, Rome, the Middle Ages, the Renaissance, and in Italian, French, English, and American literature. A short summary of translations of her work into Latin, Spanish, and German appears, also, along with a selected bibliography and twenty-four plates of sculpture, paintings, and places related to Sappho.

13. Roche, Paul. "Sappho," Greek Heritage, I (Winter, 1963), 9-15.

In this general introduction to Sappho, Roche stresses her modern sensibility, surveys her life and scholarly opinion about it, discusses the miraculous survival of her work, and closes with some general remarks on the difficulty of translating her into English. Roche's translations of ten poems by Sappho follow.

14. Sappho. Lyrics in the Original Greek with Translations, trans. Willis Barnstone. New York: New York University Press, 1965.

Barnstone's is one of the better modern translations of Sappho. His edition gives Greek text and English translation on facing pages, plus a glossary, notes, testimonia, and an index to Sappho's meters. A useful introduction precedes the poems themselves.

15. ________. Poems and Fragments, trans. Guy Davenport. Ann Arbor: University of Michigan Press, 1965.

This is another English translation. Purist Davenport disapproves of conjectural restorations, insisting on a totally unsullied text. So, he translates the poems exactly as they appear in the Greek, complete with lacunae. His pages are thus riddled with bracketed blank spaces.

16. ________. The Poems and Translations, ed. and trans. C. R. Haines. London: George Routledge & Sons, [1926].

This is an older edition of Sappho's works, with Greek text and English translation. Though supplanted by later works (notably "Lobel and Page"), Haines's work is still valuable for its introduction, which reviews her life, remaining works, character (she was innocent), the art of her poetry, and the representations of her on coins, vase paintings, and sculpture; twenty photographic plates illustrate these works. Also included are some contemporary epigrams about Sappho and a translation of Ovid's "Epistle of Sappho to Phaon."

17. ________. The Poems of Sappho, trans. Suzy Q. Groden. The Library of Liberal Arts. Indianapolis: Bobbs-Merrill Co., 1966.

This is a recent English translation of Sappho's

poems. Ms. Groden omits some fragments, so the translation is not really complete. It is, however, a fine modern rendition.

18. ________. The Poems of Sappho, with Historical & Critical Notes, Translations, and a Bibliography, ed. Edwin Marion Cox. London: Williams and Norgate, 1925.

This edition of Sappho's poems is now outdated, but still of value for the lengthy bibliography on pages 127-154.

19. ________. Sappho, ed. Max Treu. Tusculum-Bücherei. München: Heimeran, 1958.

This edition of Sappho is invaluable for the reader who knows German. It has everything in one volume: the Greek text, variant readings from the different manuscripts, notes, a German translation, an excellent bibliography, a critical study of Sappho, and ancient testimonia (what ancient writers had to say about her).

20. ________. Sappho: A New Translation, trans. Mary Barnard. Berkeley: University of California Press, 1958.

Miss Barnard has attempted to recreate in English Sappho's "fresh colloquial directness of speech." Although occasionally waxing overly-colloquial ("monkey face Atthis" and "Andromeda--that hayseed") she has produced a simple, direct translation unadorned by artificial poetic diction, in a plain style characterized by one reviewer as "pebble-like starkness."

21. ________. Sappho: Memoir, Text, Selected Renderings, and a Literal Translation, ed. and trans. Henry Thornton Wharton. New York: Brentano's, 1920.

Wharton's is a standard edition dating back into the nineteenth century, but now outdated by recent discoveries. This is a reprint of the original 1885 edition, without benefit of the four later revisions. The sixteen-page bibliography is still quite helpful for older works.

22. ________. Σαπφοῦς μέλη: The Fragments of the Lyrical Poems of Sappho, ed. Edgar Lobel. Oxford: Clarendon Press, 1925.

This is an older study, still valuable for its critical acumen and accuracy, and the lengthy introduction--a specialized linguistic examination of Sappho's dialect. The Greek text of Sappho's poems follows, although now superseded by the newer edition of Lobel and Page.

23. ________. The Songs of Sappho: Including the Recent Egyptian Discoveries; the Poems of Erinna, Greek Poems About Sappho, Ovid's Epistle of Sappho to Phaon, ed. David Moore Robinson, trans. Marion Mills Miller. New York: Frank-Maurice, Inc., 1925.

Greek texts are given, annotated by Robinson, with English translations: a literal one by Robinson, and a translation in rhymed verse by Miller. Robinson also has written an introduction on the recovery and restoration of the Egyptian relics, and a critical memoir of the real Sappho. The same procedure is followed for the Greek poems about Sappho by ancient authors, and for the poems of Erinna. An English translation of Ovid's "Epistle of Sappho to Phaon" is added at the end.

24. Weigall, Arthur. Sappho of Lesbos: Her Life and Times. New York: Frederick A. Stokes Co., 1932.

Any full-scale biography of Sappho must of necessity contain much supposition. This, one of the more ubiquitous, is no exception. It attempts to reconstruct all periods of Sappho's life: her birth and childhood, exile in Sicily, her career as a poet, life on Lesbos, relationship with her students, and her final years. Not scholarly, but popularized in approach, the book is most valuable for its overview of the social and political conditions of the time.

25. Wilamowitz-Moellendorff, Ulrich von. Sappho und Simonides: Untersuchungen über Griechische Lyriker. Berlin: Weidmann, 1913.

In this older but still major work, the author interprets the two great odes and fragments known at the time, comments extensively on the nature of Sappho's poetry, and includes one of the more important defenses championing her virtuous character.

OTHER WOMEN AUTHORS OF GREECE

26. Aldington, Richard. Medallions in Clay. New York: A. A. Knopf, 1921.

The first section of this book, pages 13-17, consists of Aldington's translation into English of the poems of Anyte of Tegea. Twenty-five short epigrams survive under her name: epitaphs, mock epitaphs for pet animals, and nature lyrics. More of her poems are still in existence than those of any other Greek poetess, says Aldington, yet she is an obscure person of whom almost nothing is certainly known. This book was reissued in London in 1930 by Chatto & Windus, under the title *Medallions from Anyte of Tegea, Meleager of Gadara, the Anacreontea, Latin Poets of the Renaissance*.

27. Athenaeus. *The Deipnosophists, Vol. 3*, trans. Charles Burton Gulick. The Loeb Classical Library. Cambridge, Mass.: Harvard University Press, 1957.

In vii, 297 of this work, Athenaeus has preserved one fragment from a poem called "Scylla" by the poetess Hedyle.

28. Barnstone, Willis (trans.). *Greek Lyric Poetry*. New York: Bantam Books, 1962.

This anthology of Greek lyric poems in English contains selected works by Sappho and some of the lesser-known poetesses (Telesilla, Corinna, Praxilla, and Anyte), rendered in a sensitive translation.

29. Bengtson, H. "Das Imperium Romanum in Griechischer Sicht," *Gymnasium*, LXXI (1964), 150-166.

This is on the conception of Rome and its empire as revealed in the writings of Melinno and others.

30. Bolling, George Melville. "Notes on Corinna," *American Journal of Philology*, LXXVII, 3 (1956), 282-287.

Extensive discussion is given to the textual problems in Corinna's fragment 1(a), which tells of a singing contest and the resulting decision arrived at by secret ballot. Bolling sets forth the parallels between the voting here and "Athenian practice," and concludes that the similarity "is strong reason for dating her *ca.* 200 B.C.," rather than the more common date two centuries earlier.

31. Bowra, C. M. "Date of Corinna," *Classical Review*, XLV (February, 1931), 4-5.

Citing holes in Edgar Lobel's argument (see number 54 below) that Corinna was not a contemporary of Pindar but lived much later, Bowra argues in support of the traditional fifth-century date.

32. ________. "Erinna's Lament for Baucis," pp. 325-342 in Greek Poetry and Life: Essays Presented to Gilbert Murray on His Seventieth Birthday, January 2, 1936. Oxford: Clarendon Press, 1936.

This is an important discussion of Erinna's Distaff, or "Lament for Baucis." The fragmentary text is given in Greek, with English translation. Explanation of the translation follows, along with critical assessment of Erinna's poetic technique. Bowra concludes that, although preserved only in small snatches, Erinna's writing compares "not unfavorably" with that of Sappho.

33. ________. "Later Elegy, Epigram, and Lyric Poetry," pp. 180-185 in New Chapters in the History of Greek Literature, ed. J. U. Powell. 3rd ed. Oxford: Clarendon Press, 1933.

The first five pages of this lengthy chapter present a preliminary discussion of Erinna's Distaff--its textual problems, language, and what we can learn from it about its author. Bowra later expanded his observations in his article, "Erinna's Lament for Baucis," cited above.

34. ________. "Melinno's Hymn to Rome," Journal of Roman Studies, XLVII (1957), 21-28.

Here is the most important article (indeed, almost the only extensive treatment at all) of Melinno's poem--an excellent literary analysis showing its reliance on ancient Greek poetical tradition, yet at the same time its unparalleled position in the history of Greek poetry. It deduces from Melinno's learned and allusive--if rather stiff--Alexandrian manner that she may have written in the first half of the second century B.C. The Greek text of the poem is given in full.

35. ________. Problems in Greek Poetry. Oxford: Clarendon Press, 1953.

This contains, in chapter X, the same essay, "Erinna's Lament for Baucis," included in Greek Poetry and Life, above. Also, chapter IV, "The Daughters of Asopus," is a full discussion of who they were and how Corinna uses them in her poem about them.

36. Cameron, Averil, and Alan Cameron. "Erinna's Distaff," Classical Quarterly, new ser., XIX (November, 1969), 285-288.

The Camerons assert that Erinna did indeed write a poem entitled the "Distaff," although some scholars have doubted it. Giving such a title to a lament for her dead friend Baucis is not really so inappropriate, they explain, because the "distaff" refers not only to the spinning of wool, but also to the spindle of the Fates.

37. Carugno, G. "Nosside," Giornale Italiano di Filologia, X (1957), 324-335.
This is a general discussion of the poetry of Nossis, noting her similarities to other Alexandrian epigrammatists and the psychological insight of some of her portraits.

38. Collart, Paul. "La Poêtesse Erinna," Comptes Rendus de l'Académie des Inscriptions et Belles-Lettres, April-June, 1944, pp. 183-199.
The author presents what little we know for sure about Erinna. He scans the remaining fragments of her work, particularly "The Distaff," to find what they can tell us about their author, and he closes with a discussion of her influence on later authors.

39. Cupaiuolo, Nice. Poetesse Greche: Corinna. Napoli: Rondinella, 1939.
This is a scholarly Italian study of Corinna's life and art, discussing her remaining fragments and her influence on Pindar.

40. Diehl, Ernst (ed.). Anthologia Lyrica Graeca. 3 vols. 3rd ed. Leipzig: B. G. Teubner, 1949-52.
Volume I contains the three remaining fragments of the enigmatic verse riddles of Cleobuline, on pages 130-131. Volume III contains the works of the elegiac poet, Semonides of Amorgos, most notably his fragment number 7 (pages 52-58), a brutal satire on the character of women, whom he compares to various animals (the sow, vixen, weasel, mare, and the "good," industrious bee). He concludes that women are the greatest evil Zeus ever created.

41. Edmonds, John Maxwell. "Erinna P.S.I. 1090," Mnemosyne, 3rd ser., VI, 2 (1938), 195-203.
This article graphically illustrates the task facing the classical scholar who tries to piece together the wretched fragments, riddled with holes, after they've been dug up. Does fragment c go with a and b, and

what about d? Edmonds offers here his reconstruction of a major fragment of Erinna's lament for Baucis, relying on such evidence as which way the papyrus fibres slant and the direction of worm-courses. At the end of the article Edmonds prints his proposed Greek text, along with an English translation.

42. ________ (ed. and trans.). Lyra Graeca: Being the Remains of All the Greek Lyric Poets from Eumelus to Timotheus Excepting Pindar. 3 vols. The Loeb Classical Library. Rev. ed. Cambridge, Mass.: Harvard University Press, 1952.

These three volumes contain the works of all the Greek lyric poets, as well as testimonia by other ancient writers about them. Volume I provides this treatment for Sappho, Volume II for Telesilla, and Volume III for Myrtis, Corinna, Charixena, Praxilla, and Theano. An English translation faces the unreliable Greek text, which is heavily restored. Indeed, Edmonds is so notorious for his "restorations" (he once added two lines totally of his own creation to the end of a poem and then translated them as Sappho's) that he has been dubbed "the only ancient Greek poet to die in the nineteenth century."

43. Giangrande, Giuseppe. "An Epigram of Erinna," Classical Review, XIX (March, 1969), 1-3.

A specialized discussion of Erinna's epigram on the tomb of her friend Baucis, this analysis of the difficulties in lines 5 and 6 notes the "elegant acuteness" of these lines.

44. Gow, A. S. F., and Denys Lionel Page (eds.). The Greek Anthology: Hellenistic Epigrams. 2 vols. Cambridge: University Press, 1965.

This scholarly collection of the Hellenistic epigrams in the Greek Anthology contains in Volume I the Greek text of, and in Volume II commentary on, the epigrams of Anyte, Erinna, Moero, and Nossis. Arrangement is alphabetical by the authors' names.

45. The Greek Anthology, trans. W. R. Paton. 5 vols. The Loeb Classical Library. Cambridge, Mass.: Harvard University Press, 1916-1918.

This is a collection of ancient Greek epigrams. By referring to the index of authors in the back of each volume, one can locate poems by the poetesses Anyte, Erinna, Moero, Nossis, and also a few attributed to

Sappho. Many other epigrams are included about them and about the other lyric poetesses who all together were hailed as earth's nine Lyric Muses. Many strongly antifeminist poems are also included, most notably by Palladas of Alexandria.

46. Guillon, Pierre. "A Propos de Corinne," Annales de la Faculté des Lettres d'Aix, XXXIII (1959), 155-168.
The author vigorously supports a later date for Corinna in Hellenistic times, not back in the fifth century B. C. He claims Pausanius is mistaken when he says Corinna competed with Pindar and won; if so, then we can better understand her otherwise inconsistent fragment criticizing the poetess Myrtis for doing the very same thing.

47. ________. "Corinne et les Oracles Béotiens: La Consultation d'Asopos," Bulletin de Correspondance Hellénique, LXXXII, 1 (1958), 47-60.
Drawing heavily on Page's seminal work, Corinna (number 58 below), Guillon discusses King Asopos' consultation of a Boeotian oracle in Corinna's poem as illustrating the local character of her poetry and reinforcing the opinion that Corinna lived in Boeotian Tanagra, to be exact, during Hellenistic times in the third century B. C., rather than the fifth.

48. Hercher, Rudolf (ed.). ʼΕπιστολογράφοι ʼΕλληνικοί: Epistolographi Graeci. Paris: Editore Ambrosio Firmin Didot, 1873.
This collection of ancient Greek letters contains on pages 603-608 several letters supposedly written by the Pythagorean philosophers Theano, Melissa, and Myia. Greek and Latin texts are printed in parallel columns on the same page.

49. Latte, Kurt. "Erinna," Nachrichten der Akademie der Wissenschaften in Göttingen, Philologisch-Historische Klasse, III (1953), 79-94.

50. Lattimore, Richmond (trans.). Greek Lyrics. 2nd ed. Chicago: University of Chicago Press, 1960.
This anthology contains selections, rendered by one of the outstanding modern translators in English, from the works of these three poetesses: three by Corinna, two by Praxilla, and nine by Sappho. A map of lyric poetry shows where they and many other lyric poets lived.

51. Lévêque, Pierre. "Les Poètes Alexandrins et Rome," L'Information Historique, XXII (March-April, 1960), 47-52.

Lévêque discusses Melinno's "Ode to Rome" (and the works of other Alexandrian poets) to indicate the interest Rome held for Alexandria during its rise to power. The complete poem is quoted (in French translation), followed by a discussion principally concerned with the question of when Melinno lived and wrote.

52. Levin, Donald Norman. "Quaestiones Erinneanae," Harvard Studies in Classical Philology, LXVI (1962), 193-204.

This is a scholarly attempt to answer several basic questions concerning the Greek poetess Erinna. Ancient testimony and her own remaining writings are examined to determine when she lived (early in the fourth century B. C.), where she came from (the island of Teos), whether she died at age nineteen (impossible to say for sure), and whether or not she wrote a poem entitled "The Distaff" (yes, she did). The article is written in English.

53. Lisi, Umbertina. Poetesse Greche: Saffo, Corinna, Telesilla, Prassilla, Erinna, Anite, Miro, Nosside, Edila, Melinno. Catania: Studio Editoriale Moderno, 1933.

Dr. Lisi examines the lives and works of the ten Greek poetesses in this little volume, to illustrate how they all expressed the feminine spirit. This is one of the few books to unite a study of all the poetesses under one cover.

54. Lobel, Edgar. "Corinna," Hermes, LXV (July, 1930), 356-365.

Lobel tackles the perennial problem of when Corinna lived and wrote. About all we can be sure of is that it was sometime between 500 and 300 B. C. A short, technical examination of the metrics, language, and spelling in her text inclines him to opt for a later date.

55. Luck, Georg. "Die Dichterinnen der Griechischen Anthologie," Museum Helveticum, XI (1954), 170-187.

This is a discussion of the epigrams of the four poetesses in the Greek Anthology (Erinna, Anyte, Moero, and Nossis), their subject matter and style.

56. Maas, Paul. "Erinnae in Baucidem Nenia," Hermes, LXIX, 2 (1934), 206-209.

Preceded by a short introduction in Latin, the author's reading of the Greek text of three fragments of Erinna's lament for Baucis constitutes the greater part of this article. A life-size tracing of one of these papyrus fragments illustrates the difficulty of deriving a text from such scraps.

57. Meunier, Mario (trans.). Femmes Pythagoriciennes: Fragments et Lettres de Théano, Périctioné, Phintys, Mélissa et Myia. Paris: L'Artisan du Livre, 1932.

This is a useful book for the study of five women who were Pythagorean philosophers. Fragments of writings by Theano, Phintys, and Perictione quoted (and so preserved) in the works of others, and some letters written by Theano, Myia, and Melissa, are all that survive. These are given here in French translation, along with notes that guide the reader to the critical opinions of others. A long introduction examines the place of these women in the context of Pythagorean philosophy and tackles the problem of the authenticity of the fragments preserved under their names.

58. Page, Denys Lionel. Corinna. Society for the Promotion of Hellenic Studies Supplementary Papers, No. 6. London: The Society for the Promotion of Hellenic Studies, 1953.

This eighty-eight page booklet contains the Greek text of Corinna's remaining fragments, edited with commentary, along with chapters on her dialect, orthography, metres, and date. Greatly increasing our knowledge of this Boeotian poetess, this is a major, scholarly work.

59. ________ (ed.). Poetae Melici Graeci: Alcmanis, Stesichori, Ibyci, Anacreontis, Simonidis, Corinnae, Poetarum Minorum Reliquias, Carmina Popularia et Convivialia Quaeque Adespota Feruntur. Oxford: Clarendon Press, 1962.

This collection of Greek lyric poetry contains the text of all of Corinna's fragments on pages 325-345. It also contains texts for Telesilla (pp. 372-74) and Praxilla (pp. 386-90), and prints on page 371 Plutarch's discussion of Myrtis. This is an authoritative text for the classical scholar, complete with critical apparatus and the testimonia of ancient authors.

60. Rose, H. J. "Pindar and Korinna," Classical Review, XLVIII (February, 1934), 8.

Pindar, the story goes, once called his rival Corinna a sow. The perpetrator of this "absurd tale" was Aelian--"one of the silliest writers who ever used Greek." The point of this short note is to show that Aelian misunderstood what he read in this case, as he is well known to have done on several other occasions, too.

61. Schubart, W. "Bemerkungen zu Sappho, Alkaios und Melinno," Philologus, XCVII (1948), 311-320.

This article contains notes on five poems by Sappho and on Melinno's poem, "To Rome."

62. Smerdel, Ton. "Parva de Nosside Poetria," Πλάτων, XVII (1965), 235-239.

The author, writing in Latin, takes a look at five of the twelve epigrams by Nossis quoted in the Greek Anthology. The epigrams are quoted in the original Greek, followed by brief commentary which stresses the lyric beauty of her poetry, the simplicity of her vocabulary and metrics, and the aesthetic rightness of her images. Smerdel admiringly sees in Nossis a lyric expression comparable to Sappho's.

63. Smyth, Herbert Weir. Greek Melic Poets. New York: Biblo and Tannen, 1963.

Smyth's anthology contains the Greek texts of some representative poems by Sappho, Erinna, Telesilla, Corinna, and Praxilla (among others). Notes in the back comment on the texts and summarize the poets' lives.

64. Thesleff, Holger (ed.). The Pythagorean Texts of the Hellenistic Period. Acta Academiae Aboensis, Ser. A: Humaniora, Vol. XXX, No. 1. Åbo: Åbo Akademi, 1965.

This is a scholarly edition, with full critical apparatus, of the Greek texts of Pythagorean writings, including the letters and fragments attributed to Melissa, Myia, Perictione, Phintys, and Theano.

65. Trypanis, C. A. "Ovid and Anyte," Classical Philology, LXV (January, 1970), 52.

Here is a brief note on a passage in Ovid's Metamorphoses which was inspired by an epigram by

Anyte, showing that he was acquainted with her works. Both are quoted in the original tongues.

66. West, M. L. "Corinna," Classical Quarterly, new ser., XX (November, 1970), 277-287.

A technical discussion of interest to, and comprehensible by, the professional scholar only, this article examines Corinna's poetry in terms of its genre, meters, contents, and dialect. From this investigation the author deduces that Corinna lived and wrote--not so early as the commonly-believed fifth century B. C., or so late as 200 B. C., as has been suggested--but rather sometime in the third century.

67. Wright, Frederick Adam (ed. and trans.). The Poets of the Greek Anthology. London: George Routledge & Sons, [1924].

Pages 77-98 of this book are devoted to a chapter on the Greek women poets. In this essay Wright introduces the reader to all the known poetesses, including English translations, though, only for those represented in the Greek Anthology. Discussed at some length are Sappho, Praxilla, Cleobuline, Erinna, Anyte, Moero, and Nossis. Mention is also made of Philaenis, Hedyle, Parthenis, and other poetesses for whom only the name remains. Wright gives little critical scrutiny to their quality as poetry; his purpose is merely to show that "in what survives of Greek women's work there is enough to prove that those critics--and there have been such--who denied women any share in imaginative creation were wrong."

68. ________. "The Women Poets of Greece," Fortnightly Review, CXIII (February, 1923), 323-333.

This article is a reprint of the chapter with the same name in the author's Poets of the Greek Anthology, listed above.

WOMEN AUTHORS OF ROME

69. Bigonzo, Giuseppe. Le Sibille e i Libri Sibillini di Roma: Cenni Critico-Storici. 2nd ed. Genova: Sordomuti, 1885.

70. Bréguet, Esther. Le Roman de Sulpicia: Élégies IV,

2-12 du "Corpus Tibullianum." Genève: Georg et Cie., 1946.

This meticulously thorough and clever dissertation laboriously sets out to prove that the elegies of Sulpicia are not by Tibullus, as is indeed generally conceded, and then offers the untenable theory that Ovid wrote them instead.

71. Cacioli, Maria R. "Adattamenti Semantici e Sintattici nel Centone Virgiliano di Proba," *Studi Italiani di Filologia Classica*, XLI (1969), 188-246.

This long article analyzes the poetical technique of Proba, a noble, cultivated matron of the fourth century A.D., in particular her use of adaptations from Vergil in her *Cento*.

72. Cartault, Augustin Georges Charles. *Le Distique Élégiaque Chez Tibulle, Sulpicia, Lygdamus*. Paris: F. Alcan, 1911.

This is a critical study of the elegiac couplet as used by Sulpicia and others.

73. Ermini, Filippo. *Il Centone di Proba, e la Poesia Centonaria Latina*. Roma: E. Loescher & Co., 1909.

74. Errico, M. T. d'. "Sull' Autenticità delle Lettere di Cornelia," *Annali della Facoltà di Lettere e Filosofia dell' Università di Napoli*, X (1962-63), 19-32.

The author argues that the fragments of letters attributed to Cornelia in the manuscripts of Cornelius Nepos are not authentic.

75. Evans, Lewis (trans.). *The Satires of Juvenal, Persius, Sulpicia, and Lucilius*. New York: Harper & Brothers, 1881.

This book contains on pages 269-279 an English translation (with fulsome notes and a short introduction on the time and the author) of the seventy-line poem commonly attributed to the later Sulpicia. A satire on the expulsion of the philosophers from Rome by Emperor Domitian, its authorship is doubted by many scholars, who consider it the inferior product of a much later period.

76. Herrmann, L. "Reconstruction du Livret de Sulpicia," *Latomus*, IX (1950), 35-47.

Herrmann attempts to determine the original make-up of the earlier Sulpicia's little book of poems and concludes that several of those usually attributed to Tibullus are actually by Sulpicia.

77. Lana, Italo. La Satira di Sulpicia: Studio Critico, Testo e Traduzione. Università di Torino, Pubblicazioni della Facoltà di Lettere e Filosofia, Vol. I, fasc. 5. Torino: Università di Torino, 1949.

78. Morel, Willy (ed.). Fragmenta Poetarum Latinorum Epicorum et Lyricorum Praeter Ennium et Lucilium. Stuttgart: B. G. Teubner, 1963.

This contains, on page 134, the one remaining fragment of the later Sulpicia's love poetry to her husband Calenus. The fragment is two lines long, a doubtful fragment quoted and attributed to her by a scholiast on Juvenal VI. 537.

79. Nepos, Cornelius. Cornelius Nepos, trans. John C. Rolfe; bound with Lucius Annaeus Florus, Epitome of Roman History, trans. Edward Seymour Forster. The Loeb Classical Library. Cambridge, Mass.: Harvard University Press, 1947.

Included among Nepos's fragments are two extracts from a letter written by Cornelia to her son Gaius Gracchus, here given both in Latin and in English translation. They indicate her primary concern for the welfare of Rome and her attempts to moderate the extremism of her son. The genuineness of Cornelia's authorship is disputed; nevertheless, the letters reveal her power and influence, especially when she reminds Gaius that all his actions "should above all be agreeable to me" and that he "should consider it impious to do anything of great importance contrary to my advice." Such a forthright statement of a woman's importance in making political decisions is rare in antiquity, but consistent with what is known of Cornelia's character.

80. Proba, Anicia Faltonia. Probae Cento; Accedunt Tres Centones a Poetis Christianis Compositi, ed. C. Schenkl. Corpus Scriptorum Ecclesiasticorum Latinorum, Vol. XVI. Vienna: Kaiserliche Akademie der Wissenschaften, 1888.

This volume contains the Latin text, with commentary, of Proba's Cento, which she compiled by putting together passages from Vergil in such a way as to retell parts of the Old and New Testament.

81. Rzach, A. (ed.). Χρησμοὶ Σιβυλλιακοί: Oracula Sybillina. Prague: [n. n.], 1891.
This book contains the Greek text of the Sibylline oracles.

82. Schlelein, Hans. De Epistolis, Quarum Fragmenta in Corneli Nepotis Libris Traduntur, Corneliae, Gracchorum Matri, Vindicandis. München: Wolf & Sohn, 1900.
This critical study of Cornelia's letters argues for their genuineness, against the opinions of many scholars. The book, written in wretched Latin, argues that the letters are genuine because they sound just like an intelligent mother reproving her son.

83. Schultess, Carl. Die Sibyllinischen Bücher in Rom. Sammlung Gemeinverständlicher Wissenschaftlicher Vorträge, Neue Folge, Heft 216. Hamburg: Verlagsanstalt und Druckerei Actien-Gesellschaft, 1895.

84. The Sibylline Oracles, trans. Milton S. Terry. New York: Hunt & Eaton, 1890.
This is a translation into English blank verse of the Sibylline oracles, based on Rzach's text (see above, number 81). It is now available in a reprint by AMS Press.

85. Thiel, J. H. "De Corneliae Epistula," Mnemosyne, LVII (1929), 347-368.

86. Sulpicia (fl. 43 B.C.). The Erotic Elegies of Albius Tibullus, with the Poems of Sulpicia Arranged as a Sequence Called "No Harm to Lovers," trans. Hubert Creekmore. New York: Washington Square Press, 1966.
Of concern here is the section beginning on page 103, "No Harm to Lovers: The Love of Sulpicia and Cerinthus as Revealed in Six Elegies by Sulpicia and Five Elegies by Tibullus." Long published with the works of Tibullus, these six short poems deal with the troubled course of Sulpicia's love for Cerinthus. Latin text and English translation are printed on facing pages. The editor intersperses with Sulpicia's work five poems by Tibullus about the same love affair.

87. ________. Tibulli Aliorumque Carminum Libri Tres, ed. John Percival Postgate. Scriptorum Classicorum Bibliotheca Oxoniensis. Oxford: The Clarendon Press, 1968.

This contains the Latin text of the elegies of Sulpicia, found near the back under III, xii-xviii.

88. Sulpicia (fl. 80 A. D.). D. Iunii Iuvenalis Satirarum Libri Quinque, Accedit Sulpiciae Satira, ed. Karl Friedrich Hermann. Leipzig: B. G. Teubner, 1894.

This volume contains the Latin text of the latter Sulpicia's satire on pages 106-108.

89. ________. "Das Klagelied der Sulpicia über die Gewaltherrschaft des Kaisers Domitian," ed. and trans. Harald Fuchs, pp. 32-47 in Discordia Concors: Festschrift für Edgar Bonjour. Basel: Helbing & Lichtenhahn, 1968.

"The Lament of Sulpicia on the Despotism of Caesar Domitian," gives the text edited with translation and commentary by Harald Fuchs. This is perhaps the newest edition available, newer, certainly, than the old nineteenth-century ones. Commentary is in German. This article has also been printed separately as a sixteen-page booklet: same publisher, same year.

Male Authors

90. Aeschylus. Aeschyli Septem Quae Supersunt Tragoediae, ed. Gilbert Murray. Rev. ed. Scriptorum Classicorum Bibliotheca Oxoniensis. Oxford: Clarendon Press, 1966.

The Greek text of all the surviving plays of Aeschylus, including the following, is printed here.

91. ________. "The Suppliant Maidens," trans. S. G. Bernardete, pp. 1-42 in Aeschylus II. The Complete Greek Tragedies, ed. David Grene and Richmond Lattimore. Chicago: University of Chicago Press, 1956.

In this, perhaps the earliest Greek play still extant, the "suppliant maidens," the fifty daughters of Danaus, have fled from Egypt to Argos to avoid being forced to marry--without their consent--their Egyptian cousins. Their plight makes clear the social status of women of the time, for under the law they had no legal right to refuse.

92. Alciphron. The Letters of Alciphron, Aelian and Philostratus, trans. Allen Rogers Benner and Francis H. Fobes. The Loeb Classical Library. Cambridge, Mass.: Harvard University Press, 1949.

Alciphron's "Letters of Courtesans" are imaginary epistles supposedly written by, to, or about several Greek hetaerae. Some are historical personages, while others are purely fictitious. All exhibit a broad spectrum of personalities--from Petale and Philumena, whose business is strictly cash-on-the-line, to passionate Thais, Myrrhina, and Lamia. Most poignant of all is Menecleides' lament for his dead mistress Bacchis. English translation and original text face each other on opposite pages, as in all Loeb editions.

93. Antiphon. "Against a Step-Mother, on a Charge of Poisoning," pp. 86-94 in The Murder of Herodes and Other Trials from the Athenian Law Courts, trans. Kathleen Freeman. London: MacDonald & Co., 1946.

Dating from some time in the latter half of the fifth century B.C., this speech is put forth by a young man who claims that his stepmother poisoned his father. As a woman was not permitted to speak in person, one of her sons offers her defense: that the murder was not intentional and the poison was thought to be only a love-philtre. The inferior lot of women in Athens can best be seen in the stepmother's accomplice, a concubine whose master had absolute control over her and was planning to sell her to a brothel.

94. Apuleius. Apulei Platonici Madaurensis Opera Quae Supersunt, ed. Rudolf Helm. 2 vols. Leipzig: B. G. Teubner, 1955-59.

The original Latin text of Apuleius' "Golden Ass" is printed here.

95. ________. The Transformations of Lucius Otherwise Known as the Golden Ass, trans. Robert Graves. New York: The Noonday Press, 1951.

Most important in this ancient picaresque novel is the beautiful tale of Cupid and Psyche in Books IV, V, and VI. This is the first myth in which a mortal woman appears as an active heroine, risking death in her heroic quest into the underworld. Also of interest are the glimpses it gives of the ancient mystic cults and their exaltation of the female. See particularly the end of the book for worship of the goddess Isis.

96. Aristophanes. Aristophanes, Vol. III, trans. Benjamin Bickley Rogers. The Loeb Classical Library. Cambridge, Mass.: Harvard University Press, 1955.

This is a handy, compact source of Lysistrata, Thesmophoriazusae, and Ecclesiazusae, with Greek text and English translation on facing pages. However, the translation is hardly the best available.

97. ________. Aristophanis Comoediae, ed. F. W. Hall and W. M. Geldart. 2 vols. Scriptorum Classicorum Bibliotheca Oxoniensis. Oxford: Clarendon Press, 1967.

Volume II contains the Greek text of Lysistrata, Thesmophoriazusae, and Ecclesiazusae.

98. ________. The Congresswomen, trans. Douglass Parker. Ann Arbor: University of Michigan Press, 1967.

This is a lively modern translation of the Ecclesiazusae. Primarily a political satire of utopian, communistic theories current in fourth-century Athens, it revolves around a takeover of the state by the women, who abolish private property, establish community feeding, and establish free communal sex. Enlivened by scatological humor and sexual high jinks, the play is scarcely a recommendation for female emancipation. One must admit, though, that the women portrayed bear little resemblance to the docile, retiring females we have learned to expect from Athens.

99. ________. Ladies' Day, trans. Dudley Fitts. New York: Harcourt, Brace, and Co., 1959.

This rolicking translation catches the spirit of the Thesmophoriazusae. At their annual festival, whose sacred rites are forbidden to men, the women of Athens try Euripides for the misogyny of his plays. In spite of its heavy ridicule of women, the play gives genuine expression to feminist complaints and ideas which may have been stirring at the time. Despite the parody one also gains an idea of the rituals of the Thesmophoria festival.

100. ________. Lysistrata, trans. Dudley Fitts. New York: Harcourt, Brace and Co., 1954.

Fitts' is one of the best modern translations. Lysistrata is the classic comedy on the war between the sexes. Urged on by their leader Lysistrata (whose name, incidentally, means Dissolver of Armies), the women of Athens go on strike. Fed up by the disastrous war raging between Athens and Sparta, they seize the treasury and deny sex to their husbands until they end the war. Their ploy succeeds, too, for by the end of the play the men, whose distress is comic, would do anything to get their women back.

101. ________. Plays: II, trans. Patric Dickinson. Oxford: University Press, 1970.

This, the second of a two-volume translation into English of all eleven of Aristophanes' surviving plays, contains Lysistrata, Thesmophoriazusae, and Ecclesiazusae.

102. Baehrens, Emil (ed.). Poetae Latini Minores, Vol. I. Leipzig: B. G. Teubner, 1879.

This book contains the little-known "Consolatio ad Liviam," pages 97-121; a short introduction in Latin precedes the work. An elegiac poem written to console Livia for the death of her son Drusus, it contains 474 lines of second-rate verbosity once ascribed to Ovid. Actually, though, the authorship is unknown, but that is just as well. For an English translation, see below, number 120.

103. Botsford, G. W., and E. G. Sihler (eds.). Hellenic Civilization. New York: Columbia University Press, 1929.

This is a sourcebook of ancient writings, giving selections which illustrate Hellenic history and culture. It is especially full in its treatment of women, valuable because it includes items hard to find elsewhere, among which are the brutal satire by misogynous Semonides of Argos, the story of Hipparchia the philosopher, and Alexis of Thurii on wives and hetaerae.

104. Cicero. "For Caelius," trans. Richmond Y. Hathorn, pp. 295-336 in The Basic Works of Cicero, ed. Moses Hadas. New York: The Modern Library, 1951.

This speech is Cicero's masterful (and successful) defense of Caelius against Clodia's accusations. Parading before the jury her harlotries, adulteries, and loose habits, he creates a striking portrait of Clodia, the "Medea of the Palatine," all the while protesting his gentlemanly reluctance to impugn her honor. "I have never thought it right," he observes, "to take up arms against a lady, especially against one whose arms are so open to all."

105. ________. M. Tulli Ciceronis Orationes, Vol. I, ed. Albert Curtis Clark. Scriptorum Classicorum Bibliotheca Oxoniensis. Oxford: Clarendon Press, [1901].

The last speech in this volume is the oration "Pro Caelio," printed in the original Latin.

106. Demosthenes. "An Illegal Union: Against Neaera," pp. 191-226 in The Murder of Herodes and Other Trials from the Athenian Law Courts, trans. Kathleen Freeman. London: MacDonald & Co., 1946.

This is the same speech as the following, translated with short commentary by Dr. Freeman.

107. ________. "In Neaeram," in Demosthenes, Vol. VI, trans. A. T. Murray. 7 vols. The Loeb Classical Library. London: William Heinemann Ltd., 1964.

This speech, probably not really by Demosthenes, is the argument used against a certain Neaera. Although a courtesan and an alien, she married Stephanus, an Athenian citizen, in defiance of the law; he then proceeded to pass off her children as his own by an Athenian wife, and he illegally married them to Athenian citizens. The frank arguments of the speech reveal the position of the non-citizen woman under the law.

108. Euripides. Euripides, trans. Richmond Lattimore et al. 5 vols. The Complete Greek Tragedies, ed. David Grene and Richmond Lattimore. Chicago: University of Chicago Press, 1955-59.

Euripides, alternately labeled a feminist and a misogynist, created more memorable female roles than any other Greek dramatist. Nearly every play is worthy of mention in this regard, but some of the most pertinent for our purposes are the following. Hippolytus contains some of the bitterest outcries of misogyny to be found anywhere in Greek literature.

Medea shows the woman betrayed who kills her own children in vengeance, and who is one of the most powerful female characters in ancient literature; moreover, the play provides a strong indictment of the social conditions, and the disregard for women, which were ultimately responsible for the tragedy. Sharply contrasted is the story of Alcestis, held up as the bravest and noblest of women because she offered to die for her husband. The Trojan Women depicts the wretched fate of women in war in "heroic" antiquity, and in the Bacchae we see (among other things) women taking a prominent role in an ancient religious cult.

109. ________. Euripidis Fabulae, ed. Gilbert Murray. 3 vols. Scriptorum Classicorum Bibliotheca Oxoniensis. Oxford: Clarendon Press, 1966-69.

The Greek texts of all the remaining plays of Euripides are printed in these three volumes.

110. Gow, A. S. F. (ed.). The Greek Bucolic Poets. Cambridge: The University Press, 1953.

This contains a prose translation, with brief introductory notes, of the Idylls of Theocritus--the same English translation as that printed in number 144, below. Poems 2, "The Sorceress," and 18, "Helen's Epithalamium," are relevant here, but most important as an indication of the greater freedom of Hellenistic women is Idyll 15. It shows two women of Alexandria; Gorgo visits Praxinoa, then they both set off for the Festival of Adonis. Openly criticizing their husbands, traveling about freely, and retorting with spirit to male criticism, these independent ladies are a far cry from the sequestered women of classical Athens.

111. Homer. Homeri Opera, ed. David B. Monro and Thomas W. Allen. 5 vols. Scriptorum Classicorum Bibliotheca Oxoniensis. Oxford: Clarendon Press, 1966.

The first two volumes, in their third edition, contain the Greek text of the Iliad. Volumes 3 and 4, in their second edition, contain the Odyssey.

112. ________. The Iliad, trans. Richmond Lattimore. Chicago: University of Chicago Press, 1951.

Although primarily a poem of war, and hence a man's poem, the Iliad offers short but moving portraits of women's life in heroic times. Briseis, Hecuba, Helen, and Andromache are portrayed with special poignancy. The polarity of proper male and female roles is already well established. As Hector tells his wife, "Go therefore back to our house, and take up your own work, /the loom and the distaff, and see to it that your handmaidens/ply their work also; but the men must see to the fighting, /all men who are the people of Ilion."

113. ________. The Odyssey, trans. Robert Fitzgerald. Garden City, N.Y.: Doubleday, 1961.

Women play a major role in the story of Odysseus' wanderings and homecoming. Clever Penelope wards off the suitors for years while Odysseus encounters Calypso, Circe, Nausicaa, and Arete. Helen also appears--back home in Sparta after the Trojan War and comfortably domesticated.

114. Juvenal. A. Persi Flacci et D. Iuni Iuvenalis, ed. W. V. Clausen. Scriptorum Classicorum Bibliotheca Oxoniensis. Oxford: Clarendon Press, 1959.

This contains the Latin text of Juvenal's Satires.

115. ________. The Satires of Juvenal, trans. Rolfe Humphries. Bloomington: Indiana University Press, 1958.

A classic of misogynist writing, Satire VI is particularly vicious, a diatribe against the whole female sex. "None of them has any shame, any sense of decency," but "high or low, their lusts are alike." Juvenal's hatred makes no distinctions; the poisoner, the lust-ridden empress who spends her nights in brothels, the virtuous Cornelia, and the learned lady who converses in Greek about literature--he reviles them all with equal virulence.

116. Lucian. "Dialogues of the Courtesans," in Lucian, Vol. VII, trans. M. D. Macleod. 8 vols. The Loeb Classical Library. Cambridge, Mass.: Harvard University Press, 1961.

On pages 355-467 occurs this collection of fifteen lighthearted dialogues of Greek courtesans. Through them we glimpse the life of the average hetaerae, on a lower plane than the brilliance of Aspasia. As they talk among themselves, we see their rivalry and friendships, loves and hates, relationships to customers and mothers, homosexuality, and the dangers of their profession.

117. Lysias. Lysias, trans. W. R. M. Lamb. The Loeb Classical Library. Cambridge, Mass.: Harvard University Press, 1960.

This contains Lysias' speech "On the Murder of Eratosthenes." Greek text and English translation are printed on facing pages.

118. ________. "On the Killing of Eratosthenes the Seducer," pp. 43-53 in The Murder of Herodes and Other Trials from the Athenian Law Courts, trans. Kathleen Freeman. London: MacDonald & Co., 1946.

In this speech written sometime near the beginning of the fourth century B. C., the defendant Euphiletus argues that his murder of one Eratosthenes was justified because this man had seduced his wife; Euphiletus, having caught them in the act, did indeed have the legal right to kill the adulterer. The narrative at the beginning of the speech paints a vivid picture of the domestic life of an Athenian couple, with a dramatic account of the discovery and murder. Once caught in adultery, as Dr. Freeman observes, the wife would automatically be divorced.

119. Maidment, K. J. (trans.). Minor Attic Orators, Vol. I. The Loeb Classical Library. Cambridge, Mass.: Harvard University Press, 1953.

The first piece in this volume is Antiphon's "Prosecution of the Stepmother for Poisoning," given in Greek and English with a short introduction. See number 93 for further discussion of this work.

120. Ovid. The Art of Love, and Other Poems, trans. J. H. Mozley. The Loeb Classical Library. Cambridge, Mass.: Harvard University Press, 1947.

Ovid's amatory poems, although obviously biased in approach, reveal much about the lives of Roman ladies at the beginning of the Roman Empire. Included in this volume is a fragment "On Painting the Face," complete with amusing recipes for facial cosmetics. "The Art of Love" is sort of a how-to-do-it manual, with advice on how to find, win, and keep a mistress, followed conversely by similar advice for the women. Then comes "The Remedies of Love," whose advice is just the opposite: how to cure yourself of love once you've succumbed to it. Lastly, this volume contains a translation of the "Consolatio ad Liviam," the poem (most likely not by Ovid at all) written in consolation for Livia on the death of her son Drusus.

121. ________. Heroides and Amores, trans. Grant Showerman. The Loeb Classical Library. London: William Heinemann, 1931.

The Latin text of these two works is given here, along with an English translation. In the Amores, however, the reader is cautioned that one whole poem, and parts of others, are omitted because "a faithful rendering might offend the sensibilities of the reader."

122. ________. The Loves, the Art of Beauty, the Remedies for Love, and the Art of Love, trans. Rolfe Humphries. Bloomington: Indiana University Press, 1957.

This is a fine, modern translation of Ovid's amatory poems.

123. ________. Ovid's Heroides, trans. Harold C. Cannon. New York: Dutton, 1971.

The Heroides, or "Letters of the Heroines," are imaginary letters from women to their lovers. Mostly they are characters from mythology and legend, but Epistle XV, "Sappho to Phaon," relates the story of Sappho's passionate but unrequited love for the boatman Phaon, which led her to leap from the Leucadian cliff to her death in the sea--a tale, no doubt, purely apocryphal.

124. Petronius. The Satiricon, ed. Evan T. Sage and Brady B. Gilleland. New York: Appleton-Century-Crofts, 1969.

This gives the Latin text of the Satyricon.

125. ________. The Satyricon and the Fragments, trans. John Sullivan. Baltimore: Penguin Books, 1965.

This is a fine translation of the Satyricon. See the following entry for full discussion.

126. ________. The Satyricon, trans. William Arrowsmith. New York: Mentor Books, 1959.

The story of the Widow of Ephesus, one of the most famous episodes in the Satyricon, aimed to show that "no woman was so chaste or faithful that she couldn't be seduced." It is an excellent example of a flourishing genre. The rest of the Satyricon is valuable for the glimpses it gives us of lower-class Roman women (Fortunata and her nouveau-riche friends, for example); most of our information otherwise is about the aristocracy.

127. Plato. Dialogues on Love and Friendship: Lysis, or Friendship, the Symposium, Phaedrus, trans. Benjamin Jowett. New York: Heritage Press, 1968.

"The Symposium" is the principal source of information on Diotima of Mantinea. At one point in this dialogue Socrates relates a conversation he had with her in which she, "a woman wise in this and in many other kinds of knowledge," instructed him in the philosophy of love.

128. ________. Platonis Opera, ed. John Burnet. 5 vols. Scriptorum Classicorum Bibliotheca Oxoniensis. Oxford: Clarendon Press, 1967.

In this collection of all the works of Plato, Volume II contains the Greek text of the "Symposium," and Volume IV the "Republic."

129. ________. The Republic of Plato, trans. Francis MacDonald Cornford. New York: Oxford University Press, 1967.

Chapter 15 contains Plato's famous assertion of the equality of women. In his ideal Republic both sexes would be educated alike, and women with the necessary abilities could become Guardians just like the men. "To conclude, then," says Plato, "there is no occupation concerned with the management of social affairs which belongs either to woman or to man, as such. Natural gifts are to be found here and there in both creatures alike." In fourth century Athens such ideas were surely revolutionary.

130. ________. The Symposium of Plato, trans. Suzy Q. Groden and ed. John A. Brentlinger. Amherst: University of Massachusetts Press, 1970.

This modern edition of the "Symposium" contains a translation by Ms. Groden and a long introduction and afterword by Brentlinger. The Diotima episode is translated on pages 78-94.

131. Pliny the Younger. Letters and Panegyricus, trans. Betty Radice. 2 vols. The Loeb Classical Library. Cambridge, Mass.: Harvard University Press, 1969.

Pliny's letters reveal a view of Roman women refreshingly different from the jaundiced views of Juvenal. His letters to and about his wife Calpurnia eloquently bespeak their mutual devotion and affection, as well as her intelligence and keen interest in literature; see especially letters IV. 19, VI. 4 and 7, VII. 5, VIII. 10 and 11, and X. 120 and 121. The esteem and concern he held for other women as well can be seen in letters IV. 21, V. 16, VI. 32, and VIII. 5. The harshness of the adultery laws against women, though the husband was forgiving, is seen in VI. 31, while letters III. 16 and VI. 24 praise the heroism of two devoted wives.

132. Plutarch. Moralia, trans. Frank Cole Babbitt. 15 vols. The Loeb Classical Library. London: William Heinemann Ltd., 1927-69.

Several books of Plutarch's Moralia are important for the study of women in antiquity. "Advice to Bride and Groom," on pages 295-343 of Volume II, counsels the subordination of wife to husband, revealing the woman's place in an ideal marriage. Volume III contains "Sayings of Spartan Women," pages 451-469, which reveal their courage and spirit, and "Bravery of Women," pages 471-581, a collection of stories about brave deeds performed by ancient women--Trojan, Persian, Etruscan, as well as Greek and Roman. Plutarch wrote them after a long conversation with Clea, a high-ranking priestess of Delphi, on the equality of the sexes. Volume IV contains "The Roman Questions" and "The Greek Questions," explanations of various customs of the ancients which throw light on the lives of women then.

133. Seneca. "Consolation to Helvia," pp. 107-136 in The Stoic Philosophy of Seneca, trans. Moses Hadas. Gloucester, Mass.: Peter Smith, 1965.

In 41 B.C. Seneca was sent off in exile to Corsica. This essay, basically an expression of Stoic fortitude in the face of grief, he wrote to his mother to console her for her loss. Helvia was, according to the portrait her son paints, a strong and virtuous woman. "Your unique jewel," he says, "your fairest beauty, which time cannot wither, your greatest glory, is your proven modesty." Some insight into the condition of Roman women at the time can be gleaned, as when Seneca recommends that Helvia apply herself to study, noting that "you have some acquaintance with all the liberal arts, though the old-fashioned strictness of my father did not allow you to master them."

134. ________. "Octavia," trans. Frank Justus Miller, pp. 851-888 in *The Complete Roman Drama, Vol. II,* ed. George E. Duckworth. New York: Random House, 1942.

Although this play has been handed down with his other tragedies, it is doubtful that Seneca was actually its author. *Octavia*, the only surviving Roman historical play, portrays the tragical divorce and murder of Octavia, stepsister and wife of Nero, in 62 A. D. As a stage drama it suffers from an excess of rhetorical bombast, particularly in Octavia's incessant bemoaning of her fate. However, as noted in Duckworth's introduction, "Both the action of the drama itself and the frequent references to the events of the preceding decade seem historically accurate."

135. ________. *Seneca's Tragedies*, trans. Frank Justus Miller. 2 vols. The Loeb Classical Library. London: William Heinemann, 1927-29.

Volume II contains the tragedy *Octavia*. Latin and English versions are printed on opposing pages.

136. Socrates Scholasticus. "The Murder of Hypatia," pp. 379-380 in *A Treasury of Early Christianity*, ed. Anne Fremantle. New York: The Viking Press, 1953.

This is an original fifth-century account of the brutal slaughter of Hypatia.

137. Sophocles. "Antigone," trans. Elizabeth Wyckoff, pp. 177-226 in *Greek Tragedies, Vol. 1*, ed. David Grene and Richmond Lattimore. Chicago: University of Chicago Press, 1960.

Antigone is one of the strongest and noblest heroines in the literature, not just of Greece, but of the world. Unflinching in her courage, she embodies the eternal conflict between the laws of the state and the dictates of a higher moral law. Following her private conscience, and thus insuring her own doom at the hands of the outraged civil authorities, she delivers a message as relevant now as the day it was written.

138. ________. Sophoclis Fabulae, ed. A. C. Pearson. Scriptorum Classicorum Bibliotheca Oxoniensis. Oxford: Clarendon Press, 1967.

This volume contains the Greek text of all of Sophocles' surviving plays.

139. Tacitus. Agrippina: A Story of Imperial Rome, ed. J. B. E. Garstang. London: G. Bell & Sons, 1938.

Selections from Tacitus' Annals XI to XIV tell the story of Agrippina the Younger. The Latin text is printed with notes and vocabulary.

140. ________. Agrippine et Néron de Tacite, ed. E. de Backer, rev. P. Laurent. 4th ed. Liège: H. Dessain, 1949.

The story of Agrippina the Younger and her son Nero is presented through selections taken from books XII-XV of Tacitus' Annals, so as to gather together, "in a coherent whole, a large slice of history." In this textbook for students, the Tacitean narrative is given in Latin and broken up into short units, complete with study questions and French translations of related passages in other authors.

141. Terence. "The Mother-in-Law," pp. 83-130 in The Brothers and Other Plays, trans. Betty Radice. Baltimore: Penguin Books, 1965.

"This is a play," says Ms. Radice in her introduction, "in which the women provide the chief interest--the two mothers, the girl, and especially the courtesan Bacchis." Indeed, the "hero"--a rapist and a cad--palls sharply in contrast to Bacchis, whose dignity and nobility make her the play's true heroine. The lack of romance in the contracting of marriages, and the relentless intensity of the double standard among the Greeks, receives eloquent confirmation in this play.

142. ________. P. Terenti Afri Comoediae, ed. Robert Kauer and Wallace M. Lindsay. Scriptorum Classicorum Bibliotheca Oxoniensis. Oxford: Clarendon Press, 1965.

The Latin text of Terence's comedies, including the above, is printed here.

143. Theocritus. The Idylls of Theokritos, trans. Barriss Mills. West Lafayette, Ind.: Purdue University Studies, 1963.

This is an excellent verse translation of the Idylls.

144. ________. Theocritus, ed. and trans. A. S. F. Gow. 2 vols. Cambridge: The University Press, 1965.

This is a scholarly edition of the works of Theocritus. The Greek text and English translation face each other on opposing pages in volume 1, following a long and learned introduction. Volume 2 contains detailed commentary on the poems. See number 110 above for a fuller discussion of the significance of Theocritus to our subject.

145. Trebellius Pollio. "Tyranni Triginta," pp. 64-151 in The Scriptores Historiae Augustae, Vol. III, trans. David Magie. The Loeb Classical Library. Cambridge, Mass.: Harvard University Press, 1954.

Trebellius is one of the primary sources of information on Zenobia. In his history of the thirty pretenders to the throne of Rome, he includes (pages 134-143) two women, Zenobia and Victoria, who aspired to the imperial purple. The sketch of Zenobia reveals her personality and career, as well as the high opinion which her opponent Aurelian held of her; Victoria, a shadowy figure, receives only a paragraph. Latin and English face each other in this dual-language edition.

146. Xenophon. Memorabilia and Oeconomicus, trans. E. C. Marchant. The Loeb Classical Library. London: William Heinemann, 1923.

Here is a dual-language edition of the Oeconomicus, a Socratic dialogue which discusses the proper management of the home and estate. In the latter part of it Socrates relates a conversation he had once with an Athenian country gentleman named Ischomachus, a humorless fellow with a regimental passion for order. Having married an ignorant fifteen-year-old girl brought up in strict seclusion, he explains how he trained her to be a good wife: as soon as he "found her docile and sufficiently domesticated to carry on conversation," he instructed her in her proper duties--to stay home, bear children, and manage the household. No doubt reflecting more of Xenophon's views than Socrates', this work is one of the most important sources of evidence for the inferior position of the Greek woman.

147. ________. Xenophon's Socratic Discourse: An Interpretation of the Oeconomicus, trans. Carnes Lord, ed. Leo Strauss. Ithaca, N.Y.: Cornell University Press, 1970.

A literal translation of the Oeconomicus by Lord is followed by Professor Strauss's lengthy commentary on the work.

MODERN WORKS

GENERAL WORKS ON WOMEN (GREECE AND ROME)

148. Abbot, Willis J. Notable Women in History: The Lives of Women Who in All Ages, All Lands, and in All Womanly Occupations Have Won Fame and Put their Imprint on the World's History. [Philadelphia: John C. Winston Co.], 1913.

The subtitle indicates this book's scope. The first fifty pages give short sketches of "a group of classic dames": Agrippina, Aspasia, Cornelia, Hypatia, Zenobia, and others. Brief summaries, the chapters give an appreciative overview of their careers and importance in history.

149. Backer, Louis de. Le Droit de la Femme dans l'Antiquité; Son Devoir au Moyen Age. Paris: Claudin, 1880.

150. Barbey d'Aurevilly, Jules Amédée. Femmes et Moralistes. Paris: A. Lemerre, 1906.

The chapters of concern here are the one about Laïs of Corinth and the chapter on "Les Femmes et la Société au Temps d'Auguste," near the end of the book.

151. Bardèche, Maurice. Histoire des Femmes: Vol. I. Paris: Stock, 1968.

One of the better histories of women written for the general reader, this well-researched book covers all aspects of woman's life. Three extensive chapters give thorough treatment to women in Greece and Rome: from early Crete and Mycenae to classical Greece (a "civilization without women"). The women of Sparta and the Hellenistic period are discussed, as are Etruscan women, then the women of Rome--in its early history, during the Republic, at the time of Augustus, and ending with summaries of the careers of several later empresses.

152. Bassermann, Lujo. The Oldest Profession: A History of Prostitution, trans. James Cleugh. New York: Stein and Day, 1968.

This is a matter-of-fact and authoritative discussion. Book I, "The Pagan Sex Market" thoroughly treats those "other women". The profession was most active in Athens and Corinth, and three classes of prostitutes existed: deikteriades (common harlots of the lowest order), auletrides (flute-players and dancers), and hetaerae (the high-class courtesans). Roman brothels are also discussed, along with strict moral censorship, chastity laws, and much more.

153. Beard, Mary R. On Understanding Women. New York: Greenwood Press, 1968.

A reprint of the original edition published in 1931, this book outlines women's role in history from primitive times to the present. Part III reviews the influence of women in the intellectual ferment of Greece and Part IV covers the women of Rome.

154. _______. Woman as Force in History: A Study in Traditions and Realities. New York: Macmillan Co., 1946.

This book is a study of the tradition that throughout history women have been a subject sex, powerless and ineffectual. Quite the contrary, says Ms. Beard, who concludes that women "have played a great role in directing human events" and have indeed been a formidable force in all of history. Her last chapter reviews that history, relating on pages 278-320 the stories of many important women in Greece and Rome. An excellent categorized bibliography supplements the work.

155. Beauvoir, Simone de. The Second Sex, trans. H. M. Parshley. New York: Bantam Books, 1970.

This classic of feminist literature, by a noted French novelist and existential philosopher, contains an important chapter on women in "Patriarchal Times and Classical Antiquity." Summing up the Greek woman's condition of "semislavery," and the Roman woman's "false emancipation," Mlle. de Beauvoir interprets the significance of private property, the family, the state, and legal restrictions in the history and condition of woman.

156. Bell, Susan Groag (ed.). Women: From the Greeks to the French Revolution. Belmont, Cal.: Wadsworth Publishing Co., 1973.

This historical anthology gathers together in one volume some important writings on the position of women in Western civilization. Selections are drawn both from contemporary authors of the time and from modern scholars; well-written introductions precede each section with background on the period. Part 1, on "Women in the Ancient World: Greece and Rome," contains passages from Plato and Aristotle, followed by modern discussions by Lacey, Balsdon, and Carcopino.

157. Berman, Kathleen. "A Basic Outline for Teaching Women in Antiquity," Classical World, LXVII (February, 1974), 213-220.

The author reviews a course on women in antiquity which she offered in the spring of 1973. Included are the course outline, the schedule of assigned readings (all primary sources), and a short bibliography of additional secondary works.

158. Birt, Theodor. Frauen der Antike. Leipzig: Quelle & Meyer, 1932.

159. Boccaccio, Giovanni. Concerning Famous Women, trans. Guido A. Guarino. New Brunswick, N.J.: Rutgers University Press, 1963.

This was first written by the great Renaissance scholar and writer in 1359. The first collection of women's biographies ever written (as the author proudly states), it contains the lives of one hundred and four women of antiquity, both mythical and real. Included here as something of a curiosity, it is sometimes unreliable as historical fact, but always a good story.

160. Briffault, Robert. The Mothers: A Study of the Origins of Sentiments and Institutions. 3 vols. New York: Macmillan Co., 1927.

The conclusions of this book are still controversial and hotly debated. Briffault was one of the first major proponents of the matriarchal theory of social evolution, that women in primitive times held the power. Though ranging the world from prehistoric times to the present, he has much to say on the matriarchal Minoans, the patriarchal degradation of women in later Greece, and the "strange combination of patriarchal institutions and matriarchal sentiment" in Rome. The work is copiously footnoted, with an outstanding two-hundred-page bibliography.

161. Bullough, Vern L., and Bonnie Bullough. The Subordinate Sex: A History of Attitudes toward Women. Urbana: University of Illinois Press, 1973.

This is perhaps the most comprehensive history yet of attitudes towards women from the ancient Egyptians and Babylonians to the present day. Chapter 3, "The Pedestal with a Base of Clay," summarizes the Greek view of women as inferior creatures, noting the sheer misogyny of most Greek literature. Chapter 4 surveys "The 'Rise' of Women and the Fall of Rome." Insisting that Roman women never achieved true equality, it denies the popular notion that they were largely to blame for the fall of Rome.

162. Burck, Erich. Die Frau in der Griechisch-Römischen Antike. München: Heimeran Verlag, 1969.

This is a comparative study of ancient Greek and Roman attitudes towards women; archaic and classical Athens is opposed to Republican and Augustan Rome. The first section discusses the sociological and legal situation of ancient women, and the second section the literary evidence.

163. Davis, Elizabeth Gould. The First Sex. Baltimore: Penguin Books, 1971.

A treasure trove of misinformation, this book sets out to "put woman back into the history books" because "her contribution to civilization has been greater than man's." Ms. Davis' chapters on "The Pre-Hellenes" and "The Women of Greece and Italy" cull together indiscriminately a vast amount of material (regardless of its reliability) to "prove" that the pre-Hellenes had "female-dominated" cultures where "men were but the servers of women," that in Rome's "gynarchic social structure" the liberated women ruled the roost, and that classical Greece was really a haven of "female emancipation."

164. Diner, Helen. Mothers and Amazons: The First Feminine History of Culture, trans. John Philip Lundin. New York: Julian Press, 1965.

This book was first published in the 1930's. The author believes that matriarchy was the rule in prehistoric society, while the patriarchal family is a comparatively recent development. She discusses the women of ancient Greece and Rome, and, contending that the Amazons were not just legendary, she describes their life and history in explicit detail. Wild theories are presented as if fact, making the book unreliable as genuine history.

165. Donaldson, James. Woman: Her Position and Influence in Ancient Greece and Rome, and Among the Early Christians. London: Longmans, Green, and Co., 1907.

In spite of its age, this work is still essential for its comprehensiveness of scope, detailed thoroughness, and unbiased objectivity. Solidly based on ancient sources, it analyzes the position of women from Homeric times to early Christianity: Spartan women, Athenian women, and Roman matrons, in relation to religion, legislation, marriage arrangements, and morals. Special attention is given to the Homeric women, to Sappho and Aspasia, and to the representation of women in the plays of Plautus.

166. Drinker, Sophie. Music and Women: The Story of Women in Their Relation to Music. New York: Coward-McCann, 1948.

Looking at woman's role in the history of music, Ms. Drinker feels that women musicians were connected from the first with the religious rites of ancient mother-goddesses, and around this theme she weaves her description of the priestess-musicians of Crete, the rites of the various Greek women's cults, the lyric poetesses, and the Roman goddess-worshipers. She tosses out controversial statements without any attempt at proof, so the book, though provocative, is unreliable.

167. Duché, Jean. Le Premier Sexe. Paris: Éditions Robert Laffont, 1972.

This book about the female sex starts with animals and proceeds through to the modern feminine revolution. Chapter 7, pages 213-260, deals with the women of Greece and Rome. Starting with the evidence of Homer, it covers the women of Crete and Mycenae, compares Sparta to Hitler's Reich, and discusses women in Athens. Turning to Rome, it begins with the Etruscans and ends with the emancipation of Roman women, which it blames for the fall of Rome.

168. Dupouy, Edmond. La Prostitution dans l'Antiquité: Étude d'Hygiène Sociale. Paris: Librairie Meurillon, 1887.

169. Ewart, Andrew. The World's Wickedest Women: Intriguing Studies of Eve and Evil through the Ages. New York: Taplinger Publishing Co., 1964.

Despite its title, this "Chamber of Female Horrors" is not really a vicious outburst of misogyny; the author has given men equal time in his companion volume, The World's Wickedest Men. He begins with the evil females of myth--the Gorgons, Amazons, and Medea--then turns to the sex lives of Sappho and the "lecherous layabouts of ancient Rome": Julia, Messalina, and Agrippina.

170. Frichet, Henry. Fleshpots of Antiquity: The Lives and Loves of Ancient Courtesans, trans. Adolph Fredrick Niemoeller. New York: The Panurge Press, 1934.

171. Gide, Paul. Étude sur la Condition Privée de la Femme, dans le Droit Ancien et Moderne et en Particulier sur le Sénatus-Consulte Velléien, Suivi du: Caractère de la Dot en Droit Romain, et De la Condition de l'Enfant Naturel et de la Concubine dans la Legislation Romaine. 2nd ed. Paris: L. Larose et Forcel, 1885.

Concerned with the legal condition of women from the most ancient antiquity to the Napoleonic Code of contemporary France, this scholarly study reviews the situation in Greece, then zeroes in on Roman law, particularly the Vellaean senatus consultum, which restricted the rights of Roman women. Two shorter monographs follow this lengthy study: one on the dowry in Roman law, and one on the legal position of concubines and illegitimate children.

172. Hardy, E. R. "Priestess in the Greco-Roman World," The Churchman, LXXXIV (Winter, 1970), 264-270.

173. Kahrstedt, Ulrich. "Frauen auf Antiken Münzen," Klio, X (1910), 261-314.

This is a study of the representations of women on ancient coins. They are separated into the following divisions: Ptolemaic queens, Seleucid queens, women in other Hellenistic states, the empresses of Rome, and the women of various vassal kingdoms of the Roman Empire. Reflections on the influence and power of these women accompany the numismatic evidence.

174. King, William C. (comp.). Woman: Her Position, Influence, and Achievement throughout the Civilized World; Her Biography, Her History, from the Garden of Eden to the Twentieth Century. Springfield, Mass.: The King-Richardson Co., 1902.

Book I of this volume deals with women before the Christian era, and Book II with those during the first four centuries A.D., to the fall of the Roman Empire. Many good, one-page sketches of the lives of individual famous women are included, which give judicious appraisals of their talents and importance.

175. Lacroix, Paul. History of Prostitution Among All the Peoples of the World, from the Most Remote Antiquity to the Present Day, trans. Samuel Putnam. 3 vols. Chicago: Pascal Covici, 1926.

This book, perhaps the most thorough treatment of the subject, delves into ancient sexual life and all its trappings in incredible detail. Chapters four through twenty-eight cover prostitution in Greece and Rome: sacred and legal prostitution in Greece, the various sorts of Greek courtesans, and prostitutes and mistresses in Rome from its foundation to the reign of Domitian.

176. Langdon-Davies, John. A Short History of Women. New York: Viking Press, 1927.

Chapter 3 in this summary of women's history discusses them in "The Ancient Civilizations: Asia, Egypt, Greece, Rome," with the thesis that women in

Greece were "cloistered slaves" and that the tremendous achievements of the Greeks were only made at the cost of the degradation of the whole female sex. To this he contrasts Roman women, who gradually obtained great freedom through the evolution of their legal position, and who consequently developed great strength of character.

177. Leipoldt, Johannes. Die Frau in der Antiken Welt und im Urchristentum. Gütersloh: Mohn, 1962.

178. Letourneau, Charles. La Condition de la Femme dans les Diverses Races et Civilisations. Paris: V. Giard & E. Brière, 1903.

This book surveys the condition of woman throughout the world, both in the past and present. Chapter 17 covers the condition of women in Greece, and chapter 18 in Rome. First is discussed the family, marriage, and divorce--in Sparta and Athens--then an assessment of women's social condition. The chapter on Roman women follows the same pattern: family and marriage, then a brief assessment of their social condition, education and character.

179. Ludovici, L. J. The Final Inequality. New York: Tower Publications, 1972.

Chapters 4 and 5 contain the author's interpretation of woman's place in ancient society, beginning with her "wholesome liberty" among the early Ionians, Etruscans, and Spartans. His depiction of Athenian women draws heavily on the writings of Seltman and Kitto (see below). Chapter 5 contains the usual summary of Roman women's gradual emancipation, as well as a description of the highly explicit rites of the all-female cults of Isis and the Bona Dea. This is a book which imparts more the author's peculiar opinions than a reliable body of information.

180. Mason, Amelia Ruth. Woman in the Golden Ages. New York: The Century Co., 1901.

This is a history of the condition of women up to the era of the salon. Half of the book deals with women in the ancient world: Sappho and other Greek poetesses, Spartan women, the vassalage of Athenian women, Rome's "new woman," and some famous women of imperial Rome.

181. Millett, Kate. Sexual Politics. Garden City, N.Y.:

Doubleday & Co., 1970.

Already a classic of the new women's movement, Ms. Millett's dissertation contains short but perceptive digressions on the implications of woman's place in Greek literature and myth: first (pages 51-52), the misogyny of the tale of Pandora, and then (pages 112-115) an analysis of Aeschylus' Eumenides as a symbolic portrayal of the triumph of patriarchy over an earlier matriarchal order.

182. Montifaud, M. A. Die Courtisanen des Alterthums. 3rd ed. Budapest: Grimm, 1902.

183. Mozans, H. J. [John Augustine Zahm]. Woman in Science: With an Introductory Chapter on Woman's Long Struggle for Things of the Mind. New York: D. Appleton and Co., 1913.

Pages 1-34 of the introductory chapter summarize the education available to the women of ancient Greece and Rome. Later chapters present woman's contribution to various branches of science, with several Greek women mentioned in relation to mathematics, astronomy, physics, and medicine.

184. Muir, Charles S. Women, the Makers of History. New York: The Vantage Press, 1956.

The author discusses women of history who have wielded great influence and power. He includes brief discussions of various women in antiquity, among whom are Aspasia, Boadicea, Zenobia, Agrippina the Younger, Cornelia, Hypatia, Messalina, Sappho, and Tomyris.

185. O'Faolain, Julia, and Lauro Martinez (eds.). Not in God's Image: Women in History from the Greeks to the Victorians. New York: Harper & Row, 1973.

This is a book of short passages taken from the writings of the time, along with commentary by the editors. Giving an introduction to the lives of women of all classes in preclassical Greece, Sparta, Athens, Hellenistic Greece, and Rome, it is a good book to find--all in one place--the most important written evidence left by the ancients.

186. Préhistoire et Antiquité. Vol. I of Histoire Mondiale de la Femme, ed. Pierre Grimal. Paris: Nouvelle Librairie de France, 1965.

For the reader who knows French, this is one of the best modern surveys of woman in the ancient past. Well-suited for the general reader by its readable style and attractive format, its intelligent approach--free from extreme biases and relying on a wide variety of ancient and modern sources--make it of service to the scholar, also. Enhanced by numerous photographs (both black-and-white and color), it offers long chapters by noted experts on women from prehistoric times to Rome. The chapters on women in Greece and Rome are individually analyzed below (see numbers 226 and 416).

187. Putnam, Emily James. The Lady: Studies of Certain Significant Phases of Her History. New York: G. P. Putnam's Sons, 1910.

This important work, recently reprinted, looks at "the lady," that is, "the female of the favoured social class." The first chapter deals with the Greek lady and her subjection, the second with the Roman lady and her greater freedom; later chapters proceed up to the slave states of the South. With quite a feminist point of view it historically outlines the place in society of the "privileged" woman, her ideals and character, her daily life, education, and marital status.

188. Reich, Emil. Woman through the Ages, Vol. I. 2 vols. London: Methuen & Co., 1908.

This is a highly readable introduction to women and their times, from Egypt to the Renaissance. Two long chapters are devoted to the women of Greece and Rome, summarizing their general position and discussing many individual women as examples.

189. Rogers, Katharine M. The Troublesome Helpmate: A History of Misogyny in Literature. Seattle: University of Washington Press, 1966.

Pages 22-55 deal with misogyny in the literature of Greece and Rome: from Hesiod to Aristotle, in Greek comedy and tragedy, Vergil, Juvenal, the Roman poets, and lesser-known writers. This is a well-documented survey of the subject, with much comment on woman's condition at the time as reflected in classical literature.

190. Schaible, Karl Heinrich. Die Frau im Altertum: Ein

Kulturgeschichtliches Bild. Karlsruhe: Braun, 1898.

191. Seltman, Charles. Women in Antiquity. New York: St. Martin's Press, [1956].

For a detailed survey of the subject, this is one of the more important--and more recent--written in English. It examines the life of women from Homeric times to Athens and Sparta, as seen through Greek art and literature; Roman women are discussed also, but only briefly. Caution is advised, however, regarding the author's extreme biases, which at times mar the book (note especially his outbursts against sex-hating Christian monastics).

192. Smith, Page. Daughters of the Promised Land: Women in American History. Boston: Little, Brown and Co., 1970.

Although most of this book treats of the history of American women, chapter 1 dwells at some length on women in Greece and Rome "because they provide a starting point for our consideration of the role and status of women."

193. Sonnet-Altenburg, Helene. Hetären, Mütter, Amazonen: Frauencharaktere aus der Antiken Welt. Heidenheim: Hoffmann, 1963.

194. Walton, F. T. "My Lady's Toilet," Greece and Rome, XV (May, 1946), 68-73.

Here is an enlightening if somewhat flippant look at the use of cosmetics, detailing the many beauty aids resorted to by ancient women, particularly those of Rome. A recipe for a facial cream recommended by Ovid is included.

195. Weigall, Arthur. Personalities of Antiquity. Garden City, N.Y.: Doubleday, Doran & Co., 1928.

This book contains chapters on Aspasia, Boadicea, and Zenobia. In a popular style Weigall writes admiringly of Aspasia and Zenobia; Boadicea, however, he treats lightly as some sort of virago who revolted fiercely because (in his theory) some Roman officer "smacked" her. His treatment of her is most unsympathetic because, as he explains, "big, golden-haired women in tight jumpers always appal [sic] me."

196. Winter, Alice Ames. The Heritage of Women. New York: Minton, Balch & Co., 1927.

The third and fourth chapters give a pleasantly popular, if rather superficial, account of women in Greece and Rome.

197. Zinserling, Verena. Women in Greece and Rome, trans. L. A. Jones. New York: Abner Schram, 1973.

The author, a classical archaeologist at the East German Friedrich Schiller University, has written a comprehensive introduction to the daily lives, status, and fashions of women in Greece and Rome; orthodox Marxist interpretation surfaces but faintly, mostly in the introduction. The chapters, though brief, are not superficial, and they cite extensively from ancient authors. Most notable, though, are the beautiful plates (black-and-white and full color) which make up the second half of the book. Lavishly illustrated, a strikingly-handsome large-format volume, this book aims more for a general audience than a scholarly one and is perhaps the most appealing, recent survey of the entire subject available in the English language.

WOMEN IN GREECE

198. Anderson, Florence Mary. Religious Cults Associated with the Amazons. New York: AMS Press, 1967.

This is a reprint of the original published in 1912. After summarizing the tradition of the Amazons in Greek legend, the author examines the religious cults with which they were associated--the cults of the Great Mother Cybele, the Ephesian Artemis, Amazonian Apollo, and Ares. She concludes that in general the Amazons worshipped primitive deities of fertility and war, whose rites were orgiastic and in which a Woman was the chief figure.

199. Arthur, Marylin B. "Early Greece: The Origins of the Western Attitude Toward Women," Arethusa, VI (Spring, 1973), 7-58.

This is an important theoretical investigation of the Greek woman's position as it related to the emergence of the Greek city-state, from the ninth to the sixth centuries B. C. Basically, Ms. Arthur concludes that throughout this period "women's social role and function did not undergo any fundamental transformation;" only the attitudes toward them changed, in conjunction with the progression from aristocracy to democracy.

200. Bader, Clarisse. La Femme Grecque: Étude de la Vie Antique. 2 vols. Paris: Didier et Cie., 1872.

Recently reprinted, this is a basic work on ancient Greek women. Volume One is concerned with the domestic life of women among the primitive Hellenes, the worship of goddesses, and the heroines of Homer. Volume Two proceeds to the historic period, covering the daily life and education of Spartan and Athenian women, the heroines of the great tragedians and of Greek history. The final chapter treats of the Greek poetesses, women authors, and lastly the female Pythagorean philosophers.

201. Barker, Albert W. "Domestic Costumes of the Athenian Woman in the Fifth and Fourth Centuries B. C.," American Journal of Archaeology, XXVI (October, 1922), 410-425.

Drawing on the evidence of Greek art, this article describes in detail the various styles of feminine dress in ancient Athens. Photographs of ancient art works and a series of simple sketches illustrate the garments described. The discussion is rather specialized, and the reader would be well advised to have a preliminary understanding of the chiton, himation, etc., before turning to this article.

202. Becker, Wilhelm Adolf. Charicles: or, Illustrations of the Private Life of the Ancient Greeks, trans. Frederick Metcalfe. London: Longmans, Green, and Co., 1880.

The second half of this book contains Excursuses on various aspects of Greek private life. The excursus on the hetaerae has been bowdlerized by the translator so as not to be "offensive to good taste." The last excursus, given in full, is a discussion of women in Greece, its conclusion being that they were regarded as a lower order of beings fit only for propagating the species. Citations of original sources are plentiful, and words objectionable to Victorian morality are tastefully left untranslated.

203. Benecke, E. F. M. Antimachus of Colophon and the Position of Women in Greek Poetry. London: Swan Sonnenschein & Co., 1896.

This is a study intended for the use of scholars, which traces the position of women in Greek poetry from the earliest authors to the Alexandrians. Only in the later poetry does a view of woman emerge which sees her as worthy of man's love, and the author's thesis is that Antimachus of Colophon was the first Greek poet to present such a theme. Similarly, the second main essay in the book traces the treatment of woman in Greek comedy.

204. Bisset, K. A. "Who Were the Amazons?" Greece and Rome, XVIII (October, 1971), 150-151.

This short article suggests that the legend of the Amazons "derives from the first encounter of Europeans with a beardless small-statured race of bow-toting mongoloids."

205. Blümner, Hugo. The Home Life of the Ancient Greeks, trans. Alice Zimmern. New York: Funk & Wagnalls Co., [1910].

Chapter IV on "Marriage and Women" and Chapter I on "Costume" are most valuable. This older book contains extensive information on the dress, education, married life, and daily routine of Greek women. It is profusely illustrated from ancient sources.

206. Bonnard, André. Greek Civilization from the Iliad to the Parthenon, trans. A. Lytton Sells. New York: Macmillan Co., 1957.

Chapter Seven discusses "Slavery and the Status of Women." The two topics are lumped together as being really the same anyway, for the Greek wife was simply the foremost among slaves. Also, Chapter V is an enthusiastic discussion of "Sappho of Lesbos, Tenth of the Muses."

207. Bonner, Robert John. "Did Women Testify in Homicide Cases at Athens?" Classical Philology, I (April, 1906), 127-132.

Generally, women were not considered competent witnesses in Athenian courts. Bonner proposes one exception to this view by pointing out a case mentioned by Demosthenes which suggests that in cases of homicide women were indeed allowed to testify.

208. Bowersock, G. W. "Some Persons in Plutarch's Moralia," Classical Quarterly, new ser., XV (November, 1965), 267-270.

This includes among other things a biographical note on Flavia Clea, the priestess of the Dionysiac Thyiads at Delphi and the woman to whom Plutarch inscribed several works.

209. Braunstein, Otto. Die Politische Wirksamkeit der Griechischen Frau. Leipzig: G. Fock, 1911.

A Ph. D. dissertation at the University of Leipzig, this work studies the women of Greece during the Roman era.

210. Bruns, Ivo. Frauenemancipation in Athen: Ein Beitrag zur Attischen Kulturgeschichte des Fünften und Vierten Jahrhunderts. Kiel: Schmidtii & Klaunigii, 1900.

211. Burger, Franz. Die Griechischen Frauen. Tusculum Schriften, No. 2. München: E. Heimeran, 1924.

212. Butler, Samuel. The Authoress of the Odyssey. Chicago: University of Chicago Press, 1967.

A reprint of the book originally published in 1897, this is an unorthodox but quite serious study arguing that the Odyssey was written, not by the Homer of the Iliad, but, over two centuries later, by a young Sicilian woman of Trapani, a headstrong, unmarried lady of the best society, but not particularly handsome.

213. Carroll, Mitchell. Greek Women. Vol. I of Woman: In All Ages and in All Countries. Philadelphia: George Barrie & Sons, 1907.

A beautiful volume printed on Japan vellum with a gold-stamped leather binding, this book is a survey for the general reader of the history of Greek womanhood from the Homeric age to Roman times; firmly based on a thorough study of ancient art, literature, and other remains, it judiciously assesses the influence and life of Greek women. Sufficient background to the age is given for the unfamiliar reader.

214. Codellas, P. S. "Ancient Greek Women Leaders in Science," pp. 226-230 in Actes du Ve Congrès International d'Histoire des Sciences, Lausanne, 1947. Paris: Académie Internationale d'Histoire des Sciences, 1948.

215. Cornish, F. Warre, and Janet Bacon. "The Position of Women," pp. 610-617 in A Companion to Greek Studies, ed. Leonard Whibley. 4th ed. Cambridge: The University Press, 1931.

This article is a useful summary of the position of women in Greece in Homeric times, at Sparta, and at Athens. Also discussed are the customs of marriage and divorce, legal status, concubines and hetaerae, the amusements allowed to women, and Greek sentiment about women. Original Greek sources are cited and interpreted.

216. Courtney, William Leonard. Old Saws and Modern Instances. London: Chapman and Hall, 1918.

The chapter on "Sappho and Aspasia," pages 89-108, gives a levelheaded survey of the lives and accomplishments of these two learned women of Greece.

217. _______. "Sappho and Aspasia," Fortnightly Review, XCVII (March, 1912), 488-495.

This is the same article as that printed above.

218. Davis, William Stearns. A Day in Old Athens: A Picture of Athenian Life. Boston: Allyn and Bacon, 1958.

Chapter V, pages 35-42, is devoted to "The Women of Athens," while later sections deal with the dress of Athenian women and the education of young girls. The author describes the arrangement of marriages, the circumscribed sphere of action and the narrow mental horizon permitted Athenian women. This is a popular account for younger readers.

219. Dickinson, G. Lowes. The Greek View of Life. 7th ed. Garden City, N.Y.: Doubleday, Doran, & Co., [1925].

This book contains two sections of interest here: a general summary of the Greek view of woman, and protests against this common view by Homer, Plato, and Euripides.

220. Dover, K. J. "Classical Greek Attitudes to Sexual Behaviour," Arethusa, VI (Spring, 1973), 59-73.

Greek attitudes toward sex are examined here. The segregation of girls and women of citizen status made it nearly impossible for young men to know or fall in love with them. The services of slaves and alien prostitutes were available, of course, but for the "satisfaction of being welcomed for his own sake by a sexual partner of equal status," the Athenian youth could turn only to members of his own sex. Hence was derived the prominence of homosexuality among the Greeks.

221. Ehrenberg, Victor. The People of Aristophanes: A Sociology of Old Attic Comedy. 3rd ed., rev. New York: Schocken Books, 1962.

In this historical and sociological account of Athenian life, chapter 8 discusses women's general seclusion, their family life and functions in the home. Evidence from the comedies of Aristophanes confirms that a woman was highly thought of only if she was a good wife, mother, and housekeeper.

222. Farina, Antonio. Il Processo di Frine. Collana di Studi Greci, Vol. 32. Napoli: Libreria Scientifica Editrice, 1959.

This is about the trial for blasphemy of the beautiful hetaera Phryne and the rather unorthodox way she gained acquittal.

223. Fitton, J. W. "'That Was No Lady, That Was...'" Classical Quarterly, new ser., XX (May, 1970), 56-66.

There is a puzzling tradition among ancient authors that Socrates had two wives. This article posits instead that Xanthippe, in spite of her prominence in stories as Socrates' shrewish wife, was not actually married to him. Rather, Socrates lived with her and had a son by her, but married a woman named Myrto sometime around 410-405 B.C.

224. Flacelière, Robert. Daily Life in Greece at the Time of Pericles, trans. Peter Green. New York: Macmillan Co., 1965.

Chapter 3 discusses the status of Greek women, their place at home, marriage rites, conjugal love (or lack of it), and family life. The author's thesis is made clear from the start: Athenian women, having no political or legal rights, were little better than slaves, confined to a sedentary existence within the walls of the women's apartments. This concise summary is supported by appropriate citations of both ancient and modern sources.

225. ________. Le Féminisme dans l'Ancienne Athènes. Paris: L'Institut de France, 1971.

Flacelière gathers together texts of the fifth century B.C. to argue that Athenian women were not really in the position of minors, and that greater liberty evolved for them during the century.

226. ________. "Histoire de la Femme Antique en Crète et en Grèce," pp. 267-374 in Préhistoire et Antiquité. Vol. I of Histoire Mondiale de la Femme. Paris: Nouveau Librairie de France, 1965.

Flacelière, in just over a hundred pages, gives a sound and sensible survey of the history of women in Minoan Crete, Mycenaean Greece, and archaic, classical, and Hellenistic Greece. The freedom of Spartan women, unique and "aberrant," he contrasts with the inferior status of Athenian women, whom he takes as representative of women in the rest of Greece. He then follows through to the gradual liberation of Greek women during the Hellenistic period.

227. ________. Love in Ancient Greece, trans. James Cleugh. New York: Crown Publishers, 1962.

This study of the Greek conception of love reveals much about the unequal position of Greek women. Greece was a firmly masculine civilization, in which respectable women by their seclusion and lack of education were incapable of spiritual or intellectual companionship with their husbands. Greek men, deprived of such relationships at home, sought them elsewhere instead, and a central tenet of this book is that the importance of pederasty and hetaerism among the Greeks is directly ascribable to this situation.

228. Fogazza, G. "Aspasia Minore," La Parola del Passato, XXV (1970), 420-422.

Through an examination of several ancient authors, Fogazza assesses the importance of Aspasia of Phocaea in history, particularly her influence at the courts of Artaxerxes II and Cyrus the Younger, his brother.

229. Forrer, Leonard. Portraits of Royal Ladies on Greek Coins. Chicago: Argonaut, 1969.

This is a numismatic study of the portraits of over fifty queens of various Hellenic kingdoms. Reproductions of most of the coins mentioned are included, along with iconographic descriptions of all of them. A brief biography of each queen precedes the listing of her coins.

230. Galt, Caroline M. "Veiled Ladies," American Journal of Archaeology, XXXV (October-December, 1931), 373-393.

The seclusion of Greek women is well known. They were supposed to stay at home, indoors. But, the author proposes, when they did go out in public they veiled their faces up to the eyes. She marshals together an impressive body of evidence to support her contention--drawing mostly on the representations of women in Greek art, primarily sculpture. Illustrations of many of these art works are liberally included.

231. Gardner, Percy. "A Female Figure in the Early Style of Pheidias," Journal of Hellenic Studies, XXXVIII (1918), 1-26.

Gardner discusses a beautiful and dignified statue of a woman, which he identifies as belonging to fifth-century Athens, in the school of the sculptor Pheidias. After comparing it to several other Greek female statues (which are plentifully illustrated by photographs), he suggests that the statue must be a portrait of Aspasia, whose importance he describes briefly.

232. Girard, Paul. Hypéride et le Procès de Phryné. Paris: B. Grasset, 1911.

This deals with Phryne's trial for blasphemy and her defense by Hyperides.

233. Godel, Roger. "Socrate et Diotime," Bulletin de l'Association Guillaume Budé, 4th ser., XIII, 4 (1954), 3-30.

This article is the same as the book of the same name described in the following citation.

234. ________. Socrate et Diotime. Paris: Société d'Edition "Les Belles Lettres," 1955.

Diotima was the learned woman from whom

Socrates himself learned the philosophy of love. Godel conjectures that she was a priestess of Apollo from Mantinea, where a line of women philosophers devoted to the search for wisdom had long flourished. He dwells at length on her religious milieu there, and how she came to influence Socrates.

235. Gomme, Arnold Wycombe. Essays in Greek History and Literature. Oxford: B. Blackwell, 1937.
The chapter on pages 89-115, "The Position of Women in Athens in the Fifth and Fourth Centuries B.C.," is a reprint of the article which appeared earlier in Classical Philology (see below).

236. ________. "The Position of Women in Athens," Classical Philology, XX (1925), 1-25.
The author suggests rather cautiously that Athenian women were perhaps not so totally subjugated as commonly supposed. He cites as evidence the dignified feminism of Attic art and drama, commenting that "there is, in fact, no literature, no art of any country, in which women are more prominent, more important, more carefully studied and with more interest, than in the tragedy, sculpture, and painting of fifth-century Athens."

237. Hadas, Moses. "Observations on Athenian Women," Classical Weekly, XXIX (February 3, 1936), 97-100.
Looking at three basic passages from Greek literature used to support the view that Athenian women were subjected to "Oriental seclusion," Hadas points out their questionable reliability and proceeds to assert that Athenian women were not really so bad off as supposed.

238. Haley, Herman W. "Social and Domestic Position of Women in Aristophanes," Harvard Studies in Classical Philology, I (1890), 159-186.
A thorough investigation of the position of Greek women as revealed in Aristophanes, taking account of the fact that he often exaggerates for comic effect, this article looks at several important passages, quoted at length in Greek. From them the author infers that the popular estimate of woman was a low one, that trust and affection between spouses was rare, and that women were generally confined to

the house. Their domestic duties are described, and also their scanty education.

239. Harrison, Jane Ellen. Prolegomena to the Study of Greek Religion. New York: Meridian Books, 1957.
Harrison was a pioneer in the study of ancient religion with the aid of anthropological data. In this book she discusses chthonic rituals and cult figures--great goddesses whose worship preceded the Olympians, and who continued into late classical times in the religious rites of the mysteries. This goddess-worship she considers as evidence of early matriarchies, and she interprets the Greek myths about the patriarchal Olympians as a record of the takeover of matriarchal civilizations and cults by patriarchal tribes. This is a reprint of the book originally published in 1903.

240. Harvey, David. "Those Epirote Women Again (SEG, XV, 384)," Classical Philology, LXIV (October, 1969), 226-229.
Although disagreeing with part of the translation put forth by Larsen in his two previous articles (see numbers 253-54 below), Harvey ends up by agreeing that the inscriptions record grants of citizenship to two women of Epirus, the purpose being in his view to serve as an honorary grant and mark of distinction.

241. Herfst, Pieter. Le Travail de la Femme dans la Grèce Ancienne. Utrecht: A. Oosthoek, 1922.
The author's doctoral dissertation, this is the most systematic and extensive investigation of the work Greek women did. The making of clothes was almost entirely in their hands, as were domestic tasks in general. Quite a few women did work outside the home as merchants, midwives, wet nurses, and, of course, prostitutes. Generally they worked because of poverty and often, especially in the case of women merchants, they had a bad reputation. In general, though, they played only an insignificant role in Greek economic life.

242. Hill, Dorothy Kent. "What the Women Did," Classical Journal, XLII (January, 1947), 202-205.
This article looks at the glimpses which Greek vase paintings give us of the everyday life of Greek

women, illustrated by photographs of several vases in the Walters Art Gallery in Baltimore. These show women busy at their daily tasks.

243. Hirvonen, Kaarle. Matriarchal Survivals and Certain Trends in Homer's Female Characters. Annales Academiae Scientiarum Fennicae, Ser. B, Vol. 152. Helsinki: Suomalainen Tiedeakatemian, 1968.

244. Holderman, Elizabeth Sinclair. A Study of the Greek Priestess. Chicago: University of Chicago Press, 1913.

This was Ms. Holderman's doctoral dissertation at the University of Michigan. Its concern is with the fact that, by and large, the Greek gods were served by priests, the goddesses by priestesses. The explanation here offered is that a very close relationship was felt to exist between god and priest, sometimes resulting in actual impersonation of the deity; so, a goddess would naturally prefer female ministrants. An appendix lists where priestesses and priests served, classified by the divinity involved.

245. Kanter, Emanuel. The Amazons: A Marxian Study. Chicago: Charles H. Kerr & Co., 1926.

This Marxian interpretation of the Amazons asserts their historical reality. They are seen as vestiges of the golden age of Primitive Communist Society, who were compelled to form a woman's state to avoid subjection to males in the patriarchal society which was then replacing the sexual equality of earlier primitive communism. Hence, they are seen as forerunners of the Proletarian Revolution.

246. Kapetanopoulos, Elias. "Klea and Leontis: Two Ladies from Delphi," Bulletin de Correspondance Hellénique, XC, 1 (1966), 119-130.

This study, based on specialized analysis of various inscriptions at Delphi, suggests that one Leontis, who is mentioned therein, was a priestess at Delphi like her acquaintance Flavia Clea, Plutarch's friend.

247. Kitto, H. D. F. The Greeks. Baltimore: Penguin Books, 1951.

In his last chapter the author suggests that the "Oriental seclusion" of Athenian women has been greatly exaggerated. He summarizes the evidence usually given to support the seclusion theory, then makes his case against this view. His argument is well-taken and worth consideration, but one must make allowance for his patronizing British bias (after all, how could the Greeks let their women attend plays "which we should certainly not allow our women to see?").

248. Kornemann, Ernst. Die Stellung der Frau in der Vorgriechischen Mittelmeer-Kultur. Orient und Antike, No. 4. Heidelberg: Winter, 1927.

249. Kowalski, G. "De Phrynes Pectore Nudato," Eos, XLII, 1 (1947), 50-62.

This article opposes the commonly-believed tradition that Hyperides laid bare Phryne's breast during her trial in order to win over the judges. It also makes general comments on the condition of courtesans in Greece.

250. Kuenen-Janssens, L. J. T. "Some Notes Upon the Competence of the Athenian Woman to Conduct a Transaction," Mnemosyne, 3rd ser., IX, 3 (1941), 199-214.

An ancient law, long cited to prove Athenian women's legal incapacity, states that they could not conclude any transactions above the value of "one medimnos of barley." The interpretation hinges on just how much a medimnos is, and the author looks at the evidence and concludes that it was a considerable amount, probably enough to feed a family of five for six days. Thus, he deduces that the Athenian woman actually had considerable freedom to conduct transactions, and the tradeswoman in the marketplace faced no special disabilities in doing business.

251. Lacey, W. K. The Family in Classical Greece. Ithaca, N.Y.: Cornell University Press, 1968.

This study of the role of the family in Greek history contains much valuable information on the status of women. Emphasis is on Homeric society, Athens, and Sparta, though other city-states in Greece are also covered. Chapter VII, on "Women in Democratic Athens," is particularly useful. The book is heavily footnoted, with numerous plates.

252. Lallier, R. De la Condition de la Femme dans la Famille Athénienne au Ve et au IVe Siècle. Paris: E. Thorin, 1875.

Although old, this is a sensible, scholarly analysis of the position of respectable married women in Athens during the fifth and fourth centuries B.C. Evidence from ancient laws, literature, and philosophy is quoted and judiciously interpreted. Acknowledging the inferior status of women, the author devotes chapters to marriage, the woman as mistress of the house, the woman in her husband's absence, adultery, divorce, widowhood, and family life.

253. Larsen, J. A. O. "Epirote Grants of Citizenship to Women," Classical Philology, LIX (April, 1964), 106-107.

Larsen deals with an inscription from the Greek city of Epirus, which he interprets as the bestowal of citizenship upon two women and their families. Such grants were apparently made freely when a citizen took a wife from a foreign community, and the author suggests that the purpose was not so much a concern with the rights of the woman as with those of her husband and his children.

254. ________. "Epirote Grants of Citizenship to Women Once More," Classical Philology, LXII (October, 1967), 255-256.

Larsen defends his translation of the inscription in his earlier article as a "perfectly clear example from the first half of the fourth century of a grant of citizenship to a woman." He reaffirms also that "the purpose of the grant seems to be to guarantee the legitimacy and citizenship of the woman's children."

255. Lewy, Henricus. De Civili Condicione Mulierum Graecarum: Commentatio ad Theodorum Thalheim. Breslau: Grassus, Barthius et Soc., 1885.

This doctoral dissertation in Latin, with extensive quotation of original Greek texts, examines the condition of Greek women under the law. All their lives they were under the tutelage of some man, a situation whose ramifications are examined in the law of obligations, laws of marriage and divorce, the dowry and the wife's own property rights, and laws relating to children and inheritance. In short, Greek women were at a distinct legal disadvantage at all times.

256. Licht, Hans [Paul Brandt]. Sexual Life in Ancient Greece, trans. J. H. Freese. New York: Barnes & Noble, 1963.

First published in 1932, this complete treatment tells everything you could possibly want to know on the subject. Hetaerae and lower classes of prostitutes are of course treated extensively, and chapter I, "Marriage and the Life of Women," examines the status of the legal wives. The author contends that Greek women were quite happy and content in their restricted homelife, because the Greeks "assigned to woman as a whole the limits which nature had prescribed for them."

257. McClees, Helen. A Study of Women in Attic Inscriptions. New York: Columbia University Press, 1920.

This doctoral dissertation discusses the life and status of women in Athens as revealed by a careful examination of ancient inscriptions (mostly sepulchral). Valuable evidence for the everyday lives of ordinary people, they reveal that women led limited, but relatively happy lives, that they did own property and engage in trade, and that in religious functions women found the most opportunities to employ their talents.

258. Macurdy, Grace Harriet. Hellenistic Queens: A Study of Woman-Power in Macedonia, Seleucid Syria, and Ptolemaic Egypt. Johns Hopkins University Studies in Archaeology, No. 14. Baltimore: Johns Hopkins University Press, 1932.

This is the most important single work which sets down the facts known about the queens of Macedonian blood who ruled in the Hellenistic kingdoms: from Eurydice, the grandmother of Alexander the Great, to Cleopatra Selene, daughter of the great Cleopatra. Many of these queens had great political power and considerably influenced the course of history; their character is also discussed, and their reputation for wickedness is refuted. This is a work of sound scholarship without rival.

259. ________. "Iotape," Journal of Roman Studies, XXVI

(1936), 40-42.

History records at least five different princesses named Iotape, coming from various little kingdoms in the eastern Mediterranean. The name apparently became dynastic in the house of Commagene, and Miss Macurdy suggests that this practice began with the Median princess Iotape, daughter of King Artavasdes, who was betrothed to a son of Mark Antony but was instead married (by arrangement of Caesar Augustus) to Mithradates III of Commagene.

260. ________. "The Political Activities and the Name of Cratesipolis," American Journal of Philology, L, 3 (1929), 273-278.

Miss Macurdy draws on ancient accounts, particularly those of Diodorus and Plutarch, to paint a vivid picture of the engaging queen Cratesipolis who, with "both beauty and brains, ... was the perfect type of the Macedonian royal woman of the end of the fourth century B. C." Her role in the complex manipulations of Macedonian politics after the death of Alexander the Great is analyzed.

261. ________. "Queen Eurydice and the Evidence for Woman Power in Early Macedonia," American Journal of Philology, XLVIII, 3 (1927), 201-214.

Miss Macurdy examines the political influence of Eurydice, Olympias, and Cleopatra, respectively the grandmother, mother, and sister of Alexander the Great. She concludes that their power resulted from their own strength of character, not from "any early tendency in the monarchy of Macedonia to exalt woman-power or as a remnant of matriarchy." Rather, the Macedonians were a strictly patriarchal people, of whom Alexander himself once said that they would not "endure to have a woman for their king."

262. ________. "Roxane and Alexander IV in Epirus," Journal of Hellenic Studies, LII (1932), 256-261.

This article reveals the complex political scheming which revolved around Alexander the Great's son and wife after his death. Rejecting the story that Roxane and her son ever fled to Epirus, Miss Macurdy summarizes at the end of the article what she believes to have happened to them, that they stayed mostly in Macedonia. Olympias, Alexander's mother, figured prominently in all the maneuverings, until all three were finally murdered, for the various regents wanted no legal heirs alive to claim the thrones they intended for themselves.

263. Mahaffy, J. P. Social Life in Greece from Homer to Menander. London: Macmillan and Co., 1894.
The author gives a lengthy discussion on the position of Greek women: their high status in Homeric times and their fall to "really Asiatic" subordination and contempt later on. The argument is supported by a detailed examination of ancient writers.

264. Michell, H. Sparta. Cambridge: The University Press, 1952.
This book contains on pages 45 through 61 a look at the strong-willed and independent women of Sparta, their marriage customs, and the unique Spartan custom of wife-sharing.

265. Mireaux, Émile. Daily Life in the Time of Homer, trans. Iris Sells. New York: Macmillan Co., 1959.
Chapter IX reviews "Homer's Women," examining the many notable women in Homer's poems and deducing from them what can be known of women then, in home and family, the customs of marriage and birth, with a timid acknowledgement of the existence of "servants of Aphrodite."

266. Möbius, Hans. "Diotima," Deutsches Archäologisches Institut Jahrbuch, XLIX, 1-2 (1934), 45-60.

267. Natorp, P. "Aischines' Aspasia," Philologus, LI (1892), 489-500.
The author attempts a reconstruction of the dialogue "Aspasia," by Aeschines the Socratic. The article is in German.

268. Nau, Abbé François (ed.). Histoire de Thaïs: Publication des Textes Grecs et de Divers Autres Textes et Versions. Paris: E. Leroux, 1903.
This book deals with the Greek hetaera, Thaïs.

269. Navarre, Octave Lucien Louis. Utrum Mulieres Athenienses Scaenicos Ludos Spectaverint Necne. Tolosae: E. Privat Bibliopola, 1900.
This Latin thesis is a scholarly examination of

the texts of ancient Greek authors to determine whether or not Athenian women were permitted to attend the theatre. The author concludes that they were.

270. Neumann, Harry. "Diotima's Concept of Love," American Journal of Philology, LXXXVI (January, 1965), 33-59.

This is a philosophical analysis of Diotima's view of love and beauty, as expressed by Socrates in the Symposium. Regarding beauty as the highest object of knowledge, she sees the goal of love as the acquisition of happiness by giving birth in or through that which is beautiful, generating in others the beauties of wisdom and virtue by a sort of psychical childbirth. This view the author labels as sophistry, taking care to distinguish it from the views usually expressed by Socrates in the dialogues.

271. Nietzsche, Friedrich. "The Greek Woman," trans. Maximilian A. Mügge, pp. 19-26 in Early Greek Philosophy & Other Essays. Volume II of The Complete Works of Friedrich Nietzsche, ed. Oscar Levy. New York: Russell & Russell, Inc., 1964.

Here is the same essay as the following, in a different translation. This is a reissue of the series originally published in 1909-1911.

272. ________. "The Greek Woman," trans. William Rose, pp. 576-579 in The World's Best Essays: From Confucius to Mencken, ed. F. H. Pritchard. New York: Halcyon House, 1939.

This short essay tells us more about Nietzsche's view of women, actually, than the Greek view. He addresses himself in particular to Plato's conception of woman and to the position allotted to women by the supreme will of the State. "The Hellenic woman," he says, "as mother, had to live in obscurity, since the political instinct, together with its highest purposes, demanded it. She had to vegetate like a plant, in a narrow circle." In such subjection "woman felt herself...in her proper position"; she was therefore glorified and "possessed more dignity than she has ever had since."

273. Notor, G. [Roton, Gabriel de]. La Femme dans l'Antiquité Grecque. Paris: Librairie Renouard, 1901.

Although aimed at a popular audience, this highly readable book is supported by extensive research and gives a complete view of the life of a Greek woman. It describes her birth, childhood, education, friendships, engagement and marriage, and family life. Details of her costume and coiffures are thoroughly illustrated, as are her occupations, amusements, and finally her funeral. Profusely illustrated by the author with line drawings based on ancient art, this is a beautiful book, striking in format and comprehensive in scope.

274. Odom, William Lee. "A Study of Plutarch: The Position of Greek Women in the First Century after Christ." Unpublished Doctor's dissertation, University of Virginia, 1961.

The author seeks to gain insight into the position of Greek women in the first century A. D. as compared with classical Athens of the fourth century B. C. To do so he examines the writings of Plutarch, which provide much information on the activities and social position of women. Detailed study confirms the subordinate status of Greek women, which Plutarch approved, though he held women in higher regard than many other Greeks.

275. ________. "Women at Athens, 490-338 B. C." Unpublished Master's thesis, University of Virginia, 1959.

276. Panayotatou, A. "Sur Quelques Femmes Intellectuelles de la Période Hellénistique," pp. 363-365 in Festschrift zum 80. Geburtstag Max Neuburgers. Wiener Beiträge zur Geschichte der Medizin, Bd. 2. Wien: W. Maudrich, 1948.

277. Paoli, Ugo Enrico. La Donna Greca nell' Antichità. Firenze: F. Le Monnier, 1953.

Fully illustrated with plates and line drawings, this study reviews the lives of Greek women--their rare appearances in public, their clothing and toilette, their childhood, marriage, and motherhood, plus a look at the life of the courtesans. This is truly a scholarly work, with seventy-six pages of footnotes.

278. Parke, H. W., and D. E. W. Wormell. The Delphic Oracle. 2 vols. Oxford: Basil Blackwell, 1956.

This is a very thorough study of the oracle at Delphi. The first volume gives its history from its origins to its demise, as well as the procedure followed by the Pythia, the prophetess. Volume II supplies the written evidence of ancient authors, printing the Greek texts of all the oracular responses.

279. Pembroke, Simon. "Last of the Matriarchs: A Study in the Inscriptions of Lycia," Journal of the Economic and Social History of the Orient, VIII (December, 1965), 217-247.

One of the main props of the theory that civilization was once matriarchal has long been a passage from Herodotus, in which he reports that the Lycians in Asia Minor used matronymics to name themselves. Pembroke examines the evidence of Lycian tomb inscriptions, which, though inconclusive, does not fully support the testimony of Herodotus. The widely-held belief in matrilineal descent among the Lycians may thus be incorrect, suggests Pembroke.

280. ________. "Women in Charge: The Function of Alternatives in Early Greek Tradition and the Ancient Idea of Matriarchy," Journal of the Warburg and Courtauld Institute, XXX (1967), 1-35.

Taking Herodotus' description of the matrilineal tracing of descent among the Lycians as a starting point, Pembroke sets out to show that this is no proof for matriarchy. By looking at the sexual customs of these and other people, and by noting how the Greeks frequently misunderstood the ways of others, he indicates that the Greeks tended to confuse matrilineal descent with the "rule of woman" (they are not the same thing), and that they often didn't know what they were talking about, anyway.

281. Perry, Walter Copland. The Women of Homer. London: William Heinemann, 1898.

This book, intended for the English reader who knows no Greek, opens with a lengthy introduction to the works of Homer and the scholarly debate surrounding them. It then launches into a summary of the position of women in Homer's poems, their married lives and dress, followed by extensive discussion of individual women and goddesses in the poems. An excursus on the later decline of women from their highly honored status in the epics closes the book.

282. Post, L. A. "The Feminism of Menander," Classical Weekly, XIX (May 3, 1926), 198-202.

After reviewing the treatment of women in the writings of earlier Greek authors, this article examines their characterization in the comedies of Menander. The author concludes that Menander was the first Greek writer to champion women; he recognized that they are not the same as men but have peculiar virtues of their own. These womanly qualities he idealized in his plays, stressing that a man who has not loved a woman devotedly and sympathetically is incomplete.

283. ________. "Woman's Place in Menander's Athens," Transactions and Proceedings of the American Philological Association, LXXI (1940), 420-459.

Drawing numerous comparisons with Athenian women and those of China, this article sets forth the position of women in Athens as deduced from the evidence of New Comedy and the prose romances. It concludes that free women were in a better position than slaves and differed from men, not in dignity or influence, but in the scope of their activities, which were generally limited to the home.

284. Préaux, Claire. "Le Statut de la Femme à l'Époque Hellénistique, Principalement en Egypte," pp. 127-175 in La Femme. Recueils de la Société Jean Bodin, Vol. XI. Bruxelles: Éditions de la Librairie Encyclopédique, 1959.

Although concentrating mostly on the women of Ptolemaic Egypt, this detailed study is valuable for an understanding of the legal position of women throughout the Hellenistic world.

285. Putnam, Emily James. "The Greek Lady," Putnam's Magazine, VII (March, 1910), 681-689; (April, 1910), 809-817.

This article on the suppression of Greek women of the upper class is the same as the second chapter of Ms. Putnam's book, The Lady (see number 187). The article also appeared in The Contemporary Review, XCVII (April, 1910), 413-428.

286. Renault, Mary. "Amazons," Greek Heritage, I (Spring, 1964), 18-23.

This is an eloquent article on the legend of the

Amazons, illustrated by photographs of Greek vase paintings. The first half summarizes the tale of Penthesilea and her Amazons in combat at Troy, as told by Arctinos, and the second looks at vestiges of fighting women in the Caucasus and elsewhere which suggest that the Amazons can not be dismissed lightly as pure myth. Long descriptive notes on the illustrations follow the essay proper.

287. Richter, Donald C. "The Position of Women in Classical Athens," Classical Journal, LXVII (October-November, 1971), 1-8.

Seeking to support the new interpretations of Gomme, Kitto, and Seltman, Mr. Richter cites passages from ancient authors to show that they have been misconstrued and that the traditional view of Athenian women's subjugation is greatly distorted. He openly challenges the orthodox view of the seclusionists, giving a panoramic survey, complete with brief quotations, of the controversy.

288. Richter, Gisela M. A. Korai: Archaic Greek Maidens. New York: Phaidon, 1968.

This is a large, lavishly-illustrated art book which studies the kore type of standing maiden in Greek sculpture. These statues of Greek women flourished throughout the archaic period of Greek art, from around 660 B.C. to around 480 B.C. Special description of the clothing, jewelry, hair styles, and footwear of the korai reveals the fashions of the times and how they changed due to political events.

289. Rose, H. J. "On the Alleged Evidence for Mother-Right in Early Greece," Folk-Lore, XXII (September, 1911), 277-291.

This article deals with the question of whether mother-right (a matrilinear system of tracing inheritance in a male-controlled society, not to be confused with female-dominant matriarchy) existed among the early Greeks. After applying "impartial criticism" to the evidence of religion, family organization, nomenclature, marriage customs, and ancient traditions, Rose finds no solid proof at all for Greek mother-right.

290. Rostovtzeff, M. "Queen Dynamis of Bosporus," Journal of Hellenic Studies, XXXIX (1919), 88-109.

An impressive bronze bust of excellent workmanship provides the starting point for this article. The author deduces that it can represent only one woman: Queen Dynamis of Bosporus. A short history of her career and her dealings with Rome ensues, followed by a summary of the fate of her dynasty after her death. A photograph of the portrait bust and of various contemporary coins illustrates the article.

291. Rothery, Guy Cadogan. The Amazons in Antiquity and Modern Times. London: Francis Griffiths, 1910.

The first sixty pages of this book give a pleasantly readable review of the legend of the Amazons among the Greeks. The tales of ancient authors are retold, and the representations of Amazons in Greek art are analyzed briefly. Sketches of various works of art illustrate the text. Later chapters go on to the legends of Amazons in more modern times around the world.

292. St. John, J. A. The History of the Manners and Customs of Ancient Greece. 3 vols. Port Washington, N.Y.: Kennikat Press, 1974.

This book was first published in 1842. The first two volumes contain a long discussion of Greek women in the heroic ages of Homer and in Sparta, followed by a look at the condition of the Athenian lady while unmarried and then (after a description of marriage ceremonies) when married. A detailed discussion of the "Toilette, Dress, and Ornaments" of Greek women closes the section. The language is at times antiquated, but much useful information can still be gleaned from the book.

293. Sainte Croix, G. E. M. de. "Some Observations on the Property Rights of Athenian Women," Classical Review, XX (December, 1970), 273-278.

This is a heavily-documented inquiry into exactly what the property rights of Athenian women were in the fourth and fifth centuries B.C. Study of inscriptions and literary sources confirms the familiar interpretation, that the women of Athens were severely restricted in their ability to own property. Even in those rare instances when a woman had nominal ownership, her kyrios (male guardian or trustee) had in reality all practical and legal control of the property. A comparison with other Hellenistic cities, where women enjoyed substantial property rights, reveals the subservient legal position of Athenian women.

294. Seltman, Charles. "The Status of Women in Athens," Greece and Rome, II (October, 1955), 119-124.
Questioning the standard view of Athenian women as despised squaws kept in Oriental seclusion, Seltman calls forth Diotima, Aristophanes, and ancient art to support his contention that Athenian women were instead held in deep respect, regard, trust, and affection.

295. Seymour, Thomas Day. Life in the Homeric Age. New York: Biblo and Tannen, 1963.
Chapter IV is devoted to "Women and the Family, Education and Recreation." The author identifies eight types of women found in Homer, represented by Helen, Andromache, Penelope, Hecuba, Arete, Nausicaa, Clytaemestra, and Euryclea. After elaborating on these eight types, and the position of the goddesses on Olympus, he reviews the marriage customs and recreations of women and concludes that women of Homeric times were clearly not kept in semi-Oriental seclusion.

296. Shear, T. Leslie. "Koisyra: Three Women of Athens," Phoenix, XVII, 2 (1963), 99-112.
This is an attempt to clear up the identity of Koisyra, an Athenian woman to whom Aristophanes makes many allusions. Three women of the same name are involved, all interrelated as members of the Alkmaionid family.

297. Shero, L. R. "Xenophon's Portrait of a Young Wife," Classical Weekly, XXVI (October 17, 1932), 17-21.
After reviewing at length passages from the Oeconomicus, the author inquires as to how much the views there expressed correspond to those of Xenophon's contemporaries. Though his approach may be stricter than most, his portrait is fairly typical: Greek girls were mere children at marriage, raised in close seclusion and kept ignorant, and they had no say in the choice of their husband. Once married, they would be at home and indoors almost all the time, with complete charge of running the household. Lastly,

there could be little intellectual companionship between husband and wife.

298. Slater, Philip E. The Glory of Hera: Greek Mythology and the Greek Family. Boston: Beacon Press, 1968.

Slater examines the influence of women in ancient Greece as revealed by their prominence in Greek mythology. From the viewpoint of Freudian psychology, he makes a detailed analysis of several myths and concludes that Greek women found power in the mother-son relationship, by which they dominated and directed the course of Greek life.

299. Sobol, Donald J. The Amazons of Greek Mythology. South Brunswick: A. S. Barnes and Co., 1972.

Part I tells the history of the Amazons as found in ancient myth and legend. Part II investigates the evidence (the accounts of the Greek historians, the images in literature and art, as well as the findings of archaeology) to come to grips with the question of whether the Amazons were myth or fact. Sobol's conclusion is that there is no incontrovertible proof either way, and maybe there never will be any. This is a readable retelling for general readers, based on secondary sources. The author is best known for his juvenile mysteries about Encyclopedia Brown.

300. Stadter, Philip A. Plutarch's Historical Methods: An Analysis of the Mulierum Virtutes. Cambridge, Mass.: Harvard University Press, 1965.

This introduction and commentary to Plutarch's "Mulierum Virtutes," a collection of anecdotes on women's brave deeds, concerns itself largely with the individual stories, summarizing them and examining their sources. The first chapter, though, briefly discusses Greek attitudes towards women and other previous collections of the actions of famous women.

301. Sumner, William Graham. "Status of Women in Chaldea, Egypt, India, Judea and Greece to the Time of Christ," Forum, XLII (August, 1909), 113-136.

This is the same article as the following.

302. ________. War, and Other Essays, ed. A. G. Keller. New Haven: Yale University Press, 1911.

This book contains on pages 65-102 an essay on the "Status of Women in Chaldea, Egypt, India, Judea, and Greece to the Time of Christ," a general summary of woman's inferior lot in antiquity. The practices of the other ancient peoples throw additional light on the situation in Greece.

303. Thiel, J. H. "De Feminarum apud Dores Condicione," Mnemosyne, LVII (1929), 193-205.

On the condition of women among the Dorians, this article states that early matriarchy seems to have maintained a certain influence over the customs of the Dorians, longer than over those of Attica. Thus, the liberty prevalent among the women of Crete is reminiscent of several aspects of Spartan customs.

304. Thompson, Maud. "The Property Rights of Women in Ancient Greece." Unpublished Doctor's dissertation, Yale University, 1906.

305. Thomson, George. The Prehistoric Aegean. Vol. I of Studies in Ancient Greek Society. London: Lawrence & Wishart, 1954.

Part Two of this volume tackles the subject of matriarchy in the prehistoric Aegean, averring that it flourished there among such peoples as the Lycians, Carians, Minoans, and Hittites, whose practices are all examined in detail.

306. Tritsch, F. J. "The Women of Pylos," pp. 406-445 in Minoica: Festschrift zum 80. Geburtstag von J. Sundwall, ed. E. von Grumach. Berlin: Akademie-Verlag, 1958.

Tritsch divides the tablets found at Pylos which have something to do with women into three groups: the first on the female slaves, the second on women's important religious functions--especially in the cult of the mother goddess--and the third, lists of women taking refuge at Pylos.

307. Tritsch, Walther. Olympias, Die Mutter Alexanders des Grossen: Das Schicksal eines Weltreiches. Frankfurt: Societäts-Verlag, 1936.

308. Tucker, T. G. Life in Ancient Athens. Chautauqua, N. Y.: The Chautauqua Press, 1917.

Chapter VIII, "Woman's Life and Fashions,"

summarizes the Athenian woman's subordinate position of seclusion, the arrangement of her marriage, her home life once married, and how she dressed. It is illustrated from ancient vase paintings.

309. Vatin, Claude. Recherches sur le Mariage et la Condition de la Femme Mariée à l'Époque Hellénistique. Bibliothèque des Ecoles Françaises d'Athènes et de Rome, Vol. CCXVI. Paris: E. de Boccard, 1970.

This thorough, scholarly volume precedes its discussion of marriage in the Hellenistic world with a general review of the situation in classical Greece. Discussion then follows of mixed marriages and the royal marriages of Hellenistic queens; marriage laws are investigated in some detail, as are nuptial customs and practices to hold down the birth rate. Throughout the work the women's perpetual tutelage is noted.

310. Vermeule, Cornelius C. "Socrates and Aspasia: New Portraits of Late Antiquity," Classical Journal, LIV (November, 1958), 49-55.

This article interprets the woman portrayed with Socrates in various decorative sculptures as Aspasia, the influential member of Athenian literary circles. It is illustrated with photographs of several sculptures.

311. Von Bothmer, Dietrich. Amazons in Greek Art. Oxford Monographs on Classical Archaeology. Oxford: Clarendon Press, 1957.

This large book is devoted to the representations (both in vase paintings and sculpture) of Amazons in Greek art of the sixth and fifth centuries B. C. Ninety pages of plates contain hundreds of different works, all representing Amazons, usually in battle. The text limits itself to iconography, however, avoiding the question of the Amazons' historical reality.

312. Wehrli, Claude. "Phila, Fille d'Antipater et Épouse de Démétrius, Roi des Macédoniens," Historia, XIII (April, 1964), 140-146.

Phila, the eldest daughter of Antipater, was a remarkable woman, noted for her intelligence, her conciliatory manners, and her generosity. Distinguished by considerable diplomatic talent, she played an important role in Macedonian politics, and this role is set forth in some detail here.

313. Wender, Dorothea. "Plato: Misogynist, Paedophile, and Feminist," Arethusa, VI (Spring, 1973), 75-90.

Plato was the most systematic feminist in the ancient world. Yet, he was also a homosexual and a misogynist. Ms. Wender quotes examples from his works to illustrate his conflicting attitudes, then offers some possible explanations. Her approach is vigorously feminist, particularly in its exposure of the "classic male chauvinism" in many Platonic passages.

314. "Were Amazons Beardless Men?" Literary Digest, May 7, 1927, pp. 26-27.

This item reports on a talk made by one Professor Myres in which he maintained that the celebrated Amazons were actually clean-shaven Hittite warriors, and not women at all. Aside from the fact that such a theory reflects poorly on the intelligence of the Greek men (ordinarily so perceptive), it contradicts the evidence of ancient writers and artists. Herodotus' tale shows just the opposite, in fact, with the Greeks first mistaking the Amazons for men and only later learning otherwise.

315. Wieth-Knudsen, K. A. Feminism: A Sociological Study of the Woman Question from Ancient Times to the Present Day, trans. Arthur G. Chater. London: Constable & Co., 1928.

The author devotes a chapter to "The Woman Question in Antiquity," which looks only at Greece. As he sees it, classical Greece was at its height when women were kept down; whereas when they became more dominant, decadence set in--"clearly" a cause-and-effect relationship. The book as a whole is a most offensive tirade, cluttered with pseudo-scholarly documentation, promoting racial as well as male supremacist notions; concludes the author, women must be put down and the "farrago of Feminism" crushed, or the white man is doomed.

316. Witton, Walter F. "The Priestess Eritha," American Journal of Philology, LXXXI, 4 (1960), 415-421.

The author takes a tablet in Mycenean script, discovered at Pylos, and transliterates it into classical Greek letters. He interprets it as a registration in verse of one Eritha's landownership claim, in which "the priestess both holds and avows holding an etonion from her deity," though in accordance with mortal law she "avows holding leases of public lands" for her property, too. The article is mostly given over to a technical, linguistic analysis of the text.

317. Wolff, Hans Julius. "Marriage Law and Family Organization in Ancient Athens: A Study on the Interrelation of Public and Private Law in the Greek City," Traditio, II (1944), 43-95.

This study of marriage laws in Athens from the pre-democratic period to the city's height contains a discussion of the personal status of married women, as well as of those women who chose "free cohabitation on a footing of equality." The position of the legal wife is summed up as follows: "The woman was, so to speak, only lent out from one family to another for the purpose of bearing offspring to maintain it."

318. Wright, Frederick Adam. Feminism in Greek Literature from Homer to Aristotle. London: George Routledge & Sons, 1923.

This is one of the most thorough discussions of the views of women expressed in Greek literature, from the misogyny of Hesiod and the lyric poets to the feminism of Euripides and Plato. The author's thesis is that the Greek world perished from one main cause: degradation of its women both in literature and social life. The book has recently been reprinted.

319. Young, Sherman Plato. The Women of Greek Drama. New York: Exposition Press, 1953.

This book, aimed at the beginning student and general reader, provides special study of the major female characters in Greek drama. Each one receives individual discussion of her strengths, weaknesses, and impact upon the play, as well as a summation of the plot.

ETRUSCAN WOMEN

320. Bachofen, Johann Jacob. Die Sage von Tanaquil, ed. E. von Kienzle. Gesammelte Werke, Vol. VI. Basel: Schwabe: 1951.

In this, one of his classic works, Bachofen argues for the existence of matriarchy in Etruscan society, giving special attention to the Etruscan wife of the first king of Rome, Tanaquil. Bachofen's argument has long been unaccepted by traditional scholars.

321. Gagé, Jean. "Tanaquil et les Rites Étrusques de la 'Fortune Oiseleuse'; de l' ἴυγξ Magique au Fuseau de Gaia Caecilia," Studi Etruschi, XXII (1952-53), 79-102.

Tanaquil, sometimes known to the Romans as Gaia Caecilia, is often represented holding a distaff. Actually, the author suggests, this distaff is not a spinning instrument at all, but a vestige of a magical object once used to attract birds for augury. He further suggests that Tanaquil was not only a magician, but originally an Etruscan goddess of Fortune.

322. Heurgon, Jacques. Daily Life of the Etruscans, trans. James Kirkup. New York: Macmillan Co., 1964.

Chapter Four, a valuable assessment of "The Etruscan Family and the Role of Women," points out the importance and freedom of Etruscan women. Investigation of the evidence of Livy's narratives, and of the contents of Etruscan tombs, confirms the unique, privileged position of the Etruscan woman, though Heurgon adds that if Etrurian society were ever a real matriarchy, it was quite diluted by the time it emerged into the light of history.

323. ________. "The Date of Vegoia's Prophecy," Journal of Roman Studies, XLIX (1959), 41-45.

Here is a scholarly examination of the prophecy supposedly delivered by the Etruscan prophetess Vegoia. The Latin text is given, and a detailed analysis follows to support the author's theory that it was issued in 91 B.C.

324. ________. "Valeurs Féminines et Masculines dans la Civilisation Étrusque," Mélanges d'Archéologie et d'Histoire de l'École Française de Rome, LXXIII (1961), 139-160.

Heurgon notes the importance of Etruscan women of the sixth century B.C., especially in the education and Hellenization of their country. Also, he comments on the modes of burial for men and for women at Caere, where the women are set apart in far more elaborate tombs than the men.

325. Slotty, F. "Zur Frage des Matriarchates bei den Etruskern," Archiv Orientâlni, XVIII (1950), 262-285.

After examining various matronymics and the evidence of inscriptions, Slotty concludes that there was not any sort of matriarchy or mother-rule among the Etruscans.

326. Warren, Larissa Bonfante. "Etruscan Women: A Question of Interpretation," Archaeology, XXVI (October, 1973), 242-249.

This is an excellent summary, freely illustrated with photographs of ancient funerary art, and aimed at the interested general reader. Stressing the independence and freedom of Etruscan women, but making no claims of matriarchy, it indicates their important legal and social position, their free public life, and their powerful role in history. The author stresses the misunderstanding of their freedom and sexual openness as lasciviousness by Greek and Roman authors used to the circumscribed lot of their own women.

327. ________. "The Women of Etruria," Arethusa, VI (Spring, 1973), 91-101.

More scholarly in style than the above, this article also reviews the status of Etruscan women, relying less, though, on ancient artifacts than on the accounts of Greek and Roman writers. Their misunderstanding of Etruscan customs is once again emphasized. Much attention is given to the wives of the Tarquins, the early Etruscan kings of Rome. Over three pages of footnotes provide a helpful guide to the bibliography of the subject.

WOMEN IN ROME AND ITS PROVINCES

328. Abbott, Frank Frost. Society and Politics in Ancient Rome. New York: Biblo and Tannen, 1963.

A reprint of the 1914 original, this book contains helpful chapters on "Women and Public Affairs Under the Roman Republic," and on "Roman Women in the Trades and Professions," in which women engaged in business, the practice of medicine, and literary pursuits are discussed. The first article reviews the role of women in the politics of the Republic: both in large bodies and in the individual influence of important women.

329. ________. "Women and Public Affairs Under the Roman Republic," Scribner's Magazine, XLVI (September, 1909), 357-366.

This is the same article reprinted in the book listed above.

330. Adcock, F. E. "Women in Roman Life and Letters," Greece and Rome, XIV (January, 1945), 1-11.

This is a well-written review of the important position of women in Roman society, their emancipation, economic independence, and political influence, with a look at the literary portraits of several individuals. It is a tightly-compressed and informative introduction, though the person who knows no Latin will miss several points.

331. Alexander, Christine. "A Portrait of Livia," The Metropolitan Museum of Art Bulletin, XI (February, 1953), 168-171.

This short article, describing a small bronze bust of a Roman lady, elderly but still a beauty, suggests that it probably represents Livia, Augustus' wife. Photographs show the bust from the front, the back, and in both profiles. The article opens with a rêsumê of Livia's life.

332. Alexander, William Hardy. "The Communiqué to the Senate on Agrippina's Death," Classical Philology, XLIX (April, 1954), 94-97.

The matricide of Agrippina the Younger by Nero was a clumsy, brutish business, and once done, it had to be explained somehow to the Senate and the Roman people. This article examines the feeble--in fact, exceptionally stupid--letter which Nero wrote to justify his crime.

333. Andrews, Ian. Boudicca's Revolt. Cambridge: The University Press, 1972.

This is a small book meant for young people, but a good introduction to life and politics in Roman Britain. Profuse illustrations, and maps unavailable elsewhere, clarify the course of the rebellion and the military strategies of each side. Boudicca herself, though, is given short shrift, basically passed off as a bad-tempered virago charging around and bellowing harshly.

334. Appleton, Charles. Trois Épisodes de l'Histoire Ancienne de Rome: Les Sabines, Lucrèce, Virginie. Paris: Librairie du Recueil Sirey, 1924.

This book recounts the story of the Sabine women, of Lucretia, and of Virginia. A criticism of various attempts to explain these episodes as mere legend, it sees in the details of the stories evidence of historical fact.

335. Assa, Janine. The Great Roman Ladies, trans. Anne Hollander. Evergreen Profile Book, No. 13. New York: Grove Press, 1960.

This is one of the more important books on the subject, fully illustrated with photographs of ancient art, as well as stills from modern motion pictures. The book focuses on the lives of noble Roman ladies from the last years of the Republic to the death of Nero. General review of their lives sets up the background of the times, against which the author narrows her discussion to the great imperial ladies of the Julio-Claudian family. Genealogies of the imperial family and a chronological table augment the usefulness of the book.

336. Austin, Lucy. "The Caerellia of Cicero's Correspondence," Classical Journal, XLI (April, 1946), 305-309.

Miss Austin tackles the problem of who the mysterious Caerellia, mentioned several times in Cicero's letters, was. A wealthy woman, to whom the orator was financially indebted and whom he was scurrilously rumored to have debauched, she was probably an Asiatic widow or divorcée who came to Rome to live, a long-time family friend who turned to Cicero for help in legal and business matters.

337. Avery, William. "Julia and Lucius Vinicius," Classical Philology, XXX (April, 1935), 170-171.

A passage in Suetonius describes how Augustus reprimanded a well-born young man named Lucius Vinicius because he came to pay his respects to Julia, the emperor's only child, at Baiae. From this incident the author deduces that Augustus tried to keep his unmarried young daughter from associating with men outside her family, because he intended to make a political match for her and wanted no romantic attachments to get in the way. Once she was married, he notes, she observed no such restrictions.

338. ________. "Julia, Daughter of Augustus: A Biography." Unpublished Doctor's dissertation, Western Reserve University, 1937.

339. Aymard, J. "Lucilla Augusta," Revue Archéologique, XXXV (1950), 58-66.

This article about Lucilla, the daughter of Marcus Aurelius and wife of Lucius Verus, his colleague as emperor, discusses--on the basis of numismatic evidence--how many children she probably had, and how her second marriage (to the aged nobody, Claudius Pompeianus) was arranged by her father in order to avoid any danger she might pose to her brother Commodus' claim to the throne.

340. Babcock, Charles L. "The Early Career of Fulvia," American Journal of Philology, LXXXVI (January, 1965), 1-32.

This is a speculative article on Fulvia's political importance before she married Mark Antony. A strong, imperious woman, politically astute, and ambitious to "rule a ruler," she maneuvered to marry three promising young men on the brink of distinguished careers. Though the situation with her first two husbands is uncertain, we know that Antony depended strongly on his wife's orders; the author, by comparing the similar careers of all three husbands, concludes that Fulvia called the shots with the first two, also, steering them along the path to prominence and power.

341. Babelon, Jean. Impératrices Syriennes. Paris: Editions Albin Michel, 1957.

This book is a comprehensive survey of the lives and accomplishments of the Syrian women (Julia Domna, Julia Maesa, and her daughters) who married into the Severan family and became empresses of Rome.

342. Bader, Clarisse. La Femme Romaine: Étude de la Vie Antique. Paris: Didier et Cie., 1877.

343. Bagnani, Gilbert. "The Case of the Poisoned Mushrooms," <u>Phoenix</u>, I, 2 (June, 1946), 15-20.
Couched in legal language as a speech spoken by counsel for the defense, this is a humorous defense of Agrippina the Younger against the charge that she killed her husband Claudius by poisoning his mushrooms. Why go to such trouble, counsel asks, when mushrooms already poisonous are available naturally? Seriously, though, examination of the evidence reveals its inconsistency. The symptoms described could be, and probably were, the result of a heart attack, instead.

344. Balsdon, John Percy Vyvian Dacre. <u>Roman Women: Their History and Habits</u>. London: Bodley Head, 1962.
Balsdon's is the most comprehensive and important book on the subject. It gives an historical account of individual Roman women as well as a general description of the public and private lives of women from all classes throughout Roman history to the death of Constantine. Copious footnotes, illustrations, and genealogical tables of the imperial families augment the usefulness of the book.

345. ________. "Women in Imperial Rome," <u>History Today</u>, X (January, 1960), 24-31.
This article gives an introduction to the extraordinary women of the early Roman Empire. Balsdon indicates the independence of these women and their conspicuous involvement in public life, concentrating especially on the careers of the powerful imperial ladies, with illustrations of portrait busts of several of them.

346. ________. "Women in Republican Rome," <u>History Today</u>, IX (July, 1959), 455-461.
This is an illustrated article on several of the notable Roman women of the late Republic. Short sketches and anecdotes introduce such women as Cornelia, Pompeia, Cato's wife Marcia, dissolute Sempronia, and Fulvia, "a Lady Macbeth of the Roman world."

347. Barini, Concetta. <u>Ornatus Muliebris: I Gioielli e le Antiche Romane</u>. Torino: Loescher, 1958.
This work examines in some detail the jewelry

worn by the women of ancient Rome. Chapters divide the subject into discussions of hair ornaments, earrings, necklaces, bracelets, rings, pins and brooches, and anklets. The book is illustrated by black-and-white mounted photographs.

348. Bartels, Heinrich. Studien zum Frauenporträt der Augusteischen Zeit: Fulvia, Octavia, Livia, Julia. München: Feder, 1963.
Here is a study of the portraiture of some important women of the Augustan era: Fulvia, Mark Antony's wife; Octavia, Augustus' sister; and Livia and Julia, his wife and daughter, respectively.

349. Bassani, Filiberto. Commodo e Marcia: Una Concubina Augusta. Venezia: Emiliana, 1905.
This book is about Marcia, the concubine of Emperor Commodus.

350. Bayer, Erich. "Die Ehen der Jüngeren Claudia Marcella," Historia, XVII (January, 1968), 118-123.
Bayer reviews the life of Marcella Claudia, the Younger, particularly the question of whom she did or did not marry. A genealogical chart is included.

351. Becker, Wilhelm Adolf. Gallus: or, Roman Scenes of the Time of Augustus, trans. Frederick Metcalfe. 2nd ed. London: Longmans, Green and Co., 1920.
In this work, first published in 1838, extensive excursuses, heavily larded with Greek and Latin quotations, describe the private life of the Romans. The first excursus includes a discussion of Roman women, in particular the wife; most of the discussion centers on the forms of Roman marriage and the ceremonies performed at weddings. A later excursus describes the dress, hair ornaments, and jewelry of Roman women.

352. Bellezza, Angela. "Cecilia Paolina," pp. 75-83 in Tetraonyma: Miscellanea Graeco-Romana. Genova: Istituto di Filologia Classica e Medioevale, 1966.
The author examines epigraphic and numismatic evidence for information on the role of Caecilia Paulina, wife of Emperor Maximinus Thrax.

353. Benario, Herbert W. "Julia Domna--Mater Senatus et Patriae," Phoenix, XII (Summer, 1958), 67-70.

"Julia Domna surpassed all other empresses of Rome in the number and variety of her titles." Such are Benario's opening words. The titles of interest here are "mother of the Senate and of the fatherland." Various inscriptions are examined in an attempt to show that Julia received these titles while her husband was still alive, not after his death.

354. ________. "The Titulature of Julia Soaemias and Julia Mamaea: Two Notes," Transactions and Proceedings of the American Philological Association, XC (1959), 9-14.

Examination of Julia Soaemias' titles indicates that her political influence may have been greater than is commonly assumed. This article also discusses when Julia Mamaea received the title "Augusta."

355. Best, Edward E., Jr. "Cicero, Livy and Educated Roman Women," Classical Journal, LXV (February, 1970), 199-204.

This reviews several Roman women praised by ancient writers. Noting their influence on their sons and husbands, the author inquires into the intellectual training of Roman women, disputing the traditional account that they were kept uneducated and domesticated at home. Instead, he suggests there was a sizable number of learned women in the late Republic and early Empire, whose influence on their sons was strong and lasting.

356. Bicknell, P. J. "Agrippina's Villa at Bauli," Classical Review, new ser., XIII (December, 1963), 261-262.

The author attempts to figure out the exact events of Agrippina the Younger's murder, particularly where she banqueted with Nero and where her villa, to which she escaped later, was located. She dined at Baiae, Bicknell avers, and after the unsuccessful attempt to drown her she fled to her villa at Bauli, which once belonged to Antonia Minor.

357. Bowen, Elizabeth. "The Virgins and the Empress," Harper's Magazine, CCXIX (November, 1959), 50-55.

This is an imaginative re-creation by a well-known novelist of the exalted and by-no-means cloistered lives of the Vestal Virgins, followed by an interpretation of the character of Livia, as suggested to Miss Bowen by the empress's villa at Prima Porta.

358. Boyancé, Pierre. "L'Apothéose de Tullia," Revue des Études Anciennes, XLVI (January-June, 1944), 179-184.

Cicero was deeply disturbed by the death of his daughter. Afterwards he many times wrote of her "apotheosis" and sought to build a sanctuary where he could pay homage to her memory. This article inquires into where Cicero may have gotten this idea.

359. Brittain, Alfred. Roman Women. Vol. II of Woman: In All Ages and in All Countries. Philadelphia: George Barrie & Sons, 1907.

Part of the same series as Carroll's book on Greek women (number 213), this also is a beautiful leather-bound volume printed on vellum. A readable survey for the general reader, it describes the women of Rome from its legendary beginnings to the accession of Constantine. The position and way of life of women in general is presented, along with short vignettes of many famous individuals.

360. Bulst, Christoph M. "The Revolt of Queen Boudicca in A.D. 60," Historia, X (October, 1961), 496-509.

This is a short scholarly survey of Boudicca and her revolt: its causes, spread, and the results when peace was reestablished. It emphasizes the revolt as an important step in the development of the Roman province of Britain.

361. Bury, J. B. "Justa Grata Honoria," Journal of Roman Studies, IX (1919), 1-13.

The princess Honoria, daughter of Galla Placidia and sister of the weak emperor, Valentinian, was self-willed and ambitious like her mother, with a spirited impatience with conventionality. When she was to be forced to marry a dully respectable senator named Herculanus, she appealed to Attila the Hun to take up her cause against her brother. He did so, claiming her as his bride and invading Italy. Bury, by pointing out an error in an ancient source, shows that Honoria committed this treasonous act when past thirty, motivated by political ambition, not as an unbridled girl of sixteen prompted by a profligate passion for a barbarian she had never seen.

362. Calderini, Aristide. Le Donne dei Severi. Donne di Roma Antica, No. 5. Rome: Istituto di Studi Romani, 1945.

Discussed here are some imperial ladies of the third century A. D. and their intrigues: Julia Domna (and how she was influenced by the Syrian worship of Baal), Julia Maesa, Julia Soaemias, and Julia Mamaea. A valuable source of information on these women, this book (unlike the others in this scholarly series) has no footnotes and, unfortunately, a bibliography of only five items.

363. Calza, Guido. "Some Portraits of Roman Empresses," Art and Archaeology, XIX (February, 1925), 93-99.

This article is illustrated with photographs of some busts discovered in ancient Ostia, which the author proposes to be portraits of Livia, Faustina the Elder, and Domitia Lucilla, the mother of Marcus Aurelius.

364. Carandini, Andrea. Vibia Sabina: Funzione Politica, Iconografia, e il Problema del Classicismo Adrianeo. Accademia Toscana di Scienze e Lettere "La Columbaria," Studi No. 13. Firenze: Leo S. Olschki, 1969.

This is a fundamental work on Hadrian's wife, emphasizing especially her iconography. Sculptural and numismatic representations are discussed at length and illustrated with over a hundred plates.

365. Carcopino, Jérôme. Daily Life in Ancient Rome: The People and the City at the Height of the Empire, trans. E. O. Lorimer. New Haven: Yale University Press, 1940.

Section IV discusses "Marriage, Woman, and the Family." The gradual decline of paternal authority and patriarchal rule is noted, followed by a summary of Roman betrothal and marriage customs. Next comes a look at the Roman matron, first at the noble women whose dignity and courage excite our admiration, then at the "unbridled" women of the Empire, whose defiance of traditional roles and morality led to the demoralization of society. The author ends with a wistful look back to the good old days when "the woman was strictly subjected to the authority of her lord and master."

366. ________. "La Véritable Julie," La Revue de Paris, LXV (January, 1958), 17-31; (February, 1958), 66-80.

Unfolding his narrative like the dénouement of a detective novel, Carcopino tells the story of Julia Major's career. His theory is that she was not the debauched profligate that ancient and modern authors have depicted. Rather, her inordinate pride and consuming lust for power were the fatal flaws which destroyed her.

367. Charlesworth, Martin P. "The Banishment of the Elder Agrippina," Classical Philology, XVII (July, 1922), 260-261.

This short note proposes a possible error in chronology. Tacitus tells us that Agrippina the Elder was banished to Pandateria, as an innocent victim of Tiberius, in 29 A. D. after Livia's death freed him from restraint. Charlesworth, on the contrary, suggests on the basis of other ancient sources that Agrippina suffered banishment while Livia was still alive, and thus that there may have been some truth in the charges of conspiracy levelled against her.

368. ________. "Livia and Tanaquil," Classical Review, XLI (May, 1927), 55-57.

Tacitus suggests that Livia poisoned Augustus in order to secure the throne for her son, Tiberius. Such a deed is unlikely; Tacitus, living long after the fact, had only rumors to go on, but he was always ready to believe the worst of the Caesars. Some authors, noting a parallel, have suggested that Tacitus was influenced by Livy's account of Tanaquil; but Charlesworth demurs, suggesting that he was more likely influenced by the alleged poisoning exploits of Agrippina the Younger.

369. Collins, John H. "Tullia's Engagement and Marriage to Dolabella," Classical Journal, XLVII (February, 1952), 164-168, 186.

In the years 51-50 B. C., Cicero was scouting around for a third husband for his daughter Tullia. During the negotiations he had to leave Italy, and in his absence Tullia married Dolabella, a disastrous choice. An examination of Cicero's correspondence reveals that he had nothing to do with this engagement, which was negotiated by his wife and daughter and to which he had to resign himself unhappily. His error, Collins concludes, was "a certain softness and over-confidence in the prudence of his wife and daughter."

370. Cook, S. A., F. E. Adcock, and M. P. Charlesworth (eds.). The Cambridge Ancient History. Vol. IX, The Roman Republic, 133-44 B.C. New York: Macmillan Co., 1932.

Most important here is the article by J. Wight Duff on "Women of the Day," pages 781-787, a largely anecdotal discussion of certain famous women during the time of Cicero. It also discusses the position of prostitutes in Rome, the proliferation of divorce in the late Republic, the considerable political influence of women, and the freedom and dignified position of the Roman matron.

371. ________. The Cambridge Ancient History. Vol. X, The Augustan Empire, 44 B.C.--A.D. 70. New York: Macmillan Co., 1934.

Chapter XIV of this book, "The Social Policy of Augustus," by Hugh Last, contains a considerable section on the position of women in Rome during the rule of that emperor. The author's attitude to "the exaggerated freedom of the womenfolk" is patronizing, but his discussion contains much of value--especially the detailed explanation of Roman marriage laws, Augustus' reform attempts to make marriage and childbearing compulsory, and the resistance to these laws.

372. ________. The Cambridge Ancient History. Vol. XI, The Imperial Peace, A.D. 70-192. New York: Macmillan Co., 1936.

A section by J. Wight Duff, "Women," pages 752-755, gives a short summary of women in Imperial Rome. He discusses the conflicting evidence: the bitter invectives of Juvenal's satire on the one hand, and the glowing picture of Pliny's wife Calpurnia on the other. Between paragon and prostitute Duff takes a moderate view of the character of most women at this time.

373. Coolidge, Julian L. "Six Female Mathematicians," Scripta Mathematica, XVII (March-June, 1951), 20-31.

The first two pages of this article summarize how little we really know about Hypatia as a mathematician, inasmuch as not one word she ever wrote remains to us. About all we can be sure of is that she was highly regarded by her contemporaries and has gone down in history as "the first mathematical martyr."

374. Corbett, Percy Ellwood. The Roman Law of Marriage. Oxford: Clarendon Press, 1930.

The standard English work on Roman marriage law, this scholarly book provides a comprehensive survey of the laws of betrothal, dowry, and marriage contracts, the forms of marriage, the status and proprietary capacity of wives, matrimonial duties and rights, and the laws governing divorce and remarriage. Much of the discussion, actually, revolves around the effects of the law on married women.

375. Corradi, Giuseppe. Cornelia e Sempronia. Donne di Roma Antica, No. 8. Rome: Istituto di Studi Romani, 1946.

This thirty-six-page study of Cornelia and her daughter Sempronia includes a genealogical table of the Scipio family. It is a scholarly work, with references to the original sources.

376. Corte, Matteo della. Loves and Lovers in Ancient Pompeii: A Pompeian Erotic Anthology, trans. A. W. Van Buren. [Rome]: E. di Mauro, 1960.

This anthology of Pompeian inscriptions and love poetry reflects much on the lives of women of the time.

377. Crook, John A. "Titus and Berenice," American Journal of Philology, LXXII (April, 1951), 162-175.

The romantic affair between Emperor Titus and his mistress Berenice, Queen of Chalcis, is here placed against the political background of 69-79 A.D., during the early years of the Flavian regime. The need to consolidate his power and conciliate those who opposed him governed when Berenice was allowed to come to Rome and when she had to be sent away.

378. Dale, M. "The Women of Imperial Rome and English Women of To-Day," Westminster Review, CXLI (May, 1894), 490-502.

This self-congratulatory article sets out to compare the women of the Roman Empire with those of the British Empire. Giving a brief summary of women in those times, its moral is that "personal enjoyment with a morbid craving for its indulgence and extreme licentiousness, the two leading motives of the lives of Roman women two thousand years ago, are not dominant characteristics of women of the superior classes in England to-day."

379. Daltrop, Georg, Ulrich Hausmann, and Max Wegner. Die Flavier: Vespasian, Titus, Domitian, Nerva, Julia Titi, Domitilla, Domitia. Das Römische Herrscherbild, II, 1. Berlin: Mann, 1966.

This is an iconographic study of the sculptured portraits of the Flavian emperors and royal women; the wives of Vespasian and Domitian, and Julia, the daughter of Titus, are discussed. Essays give detailed analyses of the portraits (both genuine and spurious), followed by catalogues of all of them and numerous plates with excellent reproductions of many of them.

380. D'Avino, Michele. The Women of Pompeii, trans. Monica Hope Jones and Luigi Nusco. Napoli: Loffredo, 1967.

This work makes available for a popular audience an extended look at the women of ancient Pompeii. Drawing largely on the inscriptions and graffiti brought to light there, D'Avino discusses working women, "women of ill-fame," housewives, menials, matrons, women involved in the mystery rites, and the involvement of Pompeian women in politics; prominent individuals receive special treatment.

381. Davis, William Stearns. A Day in Old Rome: A Picture of Roman Life. Boston: Allyn and Bacon, 1925.

In this book, a popular approach with a school textbook format, Chapter IV gives a summary of "Roman Women and Roman Marriages." After listing women's many legal disabilities the author quips, "Yet, what of it?" and goes on to call imperial Rome "a feminine paradise." In spite of this and other curious notions (Rome, for example, was a "hundred per cent civilization," whereas Athens was only a "fifty per cent civilization"), a fairly straightforward overview of Roman marriage customs follows.

382. Dawson, Alexis. "Whatever Happened to Lady Agrippina?" Classical Journal, LXIV (March, 1969), 253-267.

Tacitus' dramatic account of Agrippina's murder--the boat rigged to drown her, the more successful stabbing at her villa--is here denounced as an example of "Tacitean chicanery," and "a farrago of lies and absurdities." Instead, as Nero reported to the Senate, Agrippina had attempted that night to kill her son; then, unsuccessful, she returned to her villa and straightway stabbed herself.

383. Deckman, Alice A. "Livia Augusta," Classical Weekly, XIX (October 19, 1925), 21-25.

This short sketch reviews Livia's life and defends her against the various charges of murder and treachery levelled against her. Livia was instead a virtuous, intelligent, and politically astute woman who exercised a needed restraining influence upon her husband, Augustus.

384. Deutsch, Monroe E. "Caesar's First Wife," Classical Philology, XII (January, 1917), 93-96.

This article argues that Cossutia was Julius Caesar's first wife, and that a mistranslation of Suetonius is responsible for the generally-accepted view that she was only engaged to him and that he broke the engagement. Deutsch postulates that Caesar did indeed marry her, probably when he was fourteen years old, and that about a year later he divorced her.

385. ________. "The Women of Caesar's Family," Classical Journal, XIII (April, 1918), 502-514.

Julius Caesar's female relatives are the subject of this article. His feelings about them are suggested, to the extent that they are known, along with a summary of their lives. The women mentioned here are his mother Aurelia, his wives (Cossutia, Cornelia, Pompeia, and Calpurnia), his sisters (two Julias), and his daughter (also named Julia).

386. Dill, Samuel. Roman Society from Nero to Marcus Aurelius. London: Macmillan and Co., 1925.

Professor Dill has much to say about women and their emancipation during the first two centuries of the Roman Empire. On pages 76-87 he gives Juvenal's satire on women a judicious appraisal, using illustrations from other ancient writers to show Juvenal's exaggerated rhetoric and prejudice. He concludes that women of the time were really no more depraved than at any other time.

387. Dorey, T. A. "Adultery and Propaganda in the Early Roman Empire," University of Birmingham Historical Journal, VIII, 1 (1961), 1-6.

The article looks particularly at the lives of Agrippina the Younger, Messalina, and Julia Major; although certainly dissolute, they were no worse than many others of their time. Dorey concludes that such scandal became attached to them as the result of propaganda put out by their political enemies.

388. ________. "Cicero, Clodia and the Pro Caelio," Greece and Rome, 2nd ser., V, 2 (1958), 175-180.

The author argues that Clodia's role in the Caelius affair was strictly secondary, and that only Cicero's oratory makes us think otherwise.

389. Downey, G. "Aurelian's Victory over Zenobia at Immae, A.D. 272," Transactions and Proceedings of the American Philological Association, LXXXI (1950), 57-68.

This is a military account of the final battle in which Zenobia was defeated, based on the detailed account of Zosimus and study of the area's geography.

390. Dudley, Donald R. "The Rebellion of Boudicca," History Today, X (June, 1960), 387-394.

A concise summary of Boudicca's rebellion and the Roman abuses which provoked it, this article assesses Boudicca's central role as war-leader of the confederated British forces. It stresses the humane and more enlightened government which followed the revolt.

391. ________, and Graham Webster. The Rebellion of Boudicca. New York: Barnes & Noble, Inc., 1962.

This is the major book on Boadicea. A work

of solid scholarship, it examines the accounts of her rebellion in light of the evidence yielded by modern archaeology. After explanation of the tribal and military situation of Celtic Britain, the course of the rebellion and its aftermath is explored. A summary of the treatment of Boadicea in later histories and literature, the narrative of Tacitus in Latin and English translation, and other appendices add to the value of the book.

392. Duke, T. T. "Women and Pygmies in the Roman Arena," Classical Journal, L (February, 1955), 223-224.

Women often appeared as combatants in gladiatorial contests. Some have held that they were matched with male adversaries: pygmies, perhaps, or even full-grown men. The message of this short note, supported by close scrutiny of ancient evidence, is that such a notion is erroneous and that women in the Roman arena fought only with each other.

393. Durry, Marcel. Eloge Funèbre d'une Matrone Romaine (Eloge Dit de Turia). Paris: Société d'Edition "Les Belles Lettres," 1950.

This is a scholarly edition of the "Laudatio Turiae," the eulogy inscribed on the tomb of the Roman matron, Turia. The Latin text, with critical apparatus and French translation, is given along with commentary by Durry. He reviews the history of the *laudatio funebris* in general and Turia's *laudatio* in particular, adding his own laudatory observations on this heroic and virtuous woman.

394. Esdaile, Katharine A. "The Aged Livia," Journal of Roman Studies, IV (1914), 139-141.

Livia was one of the few women of the imperial family, during the Julio-Claudian period, to live past seventy. This article suggests that the head on a famous statue known as the "Seated Agrippina" is rather the only existing portrait of the aged Livia which realistically depicts her as an elderly, though dignified, woman. Reproductions of this and other known portraits of Livia serve to illustrate the likeness.

395. Ferrero, Guglielmo. Characters and Events of Roman History from Caesar to Nero, trans. F. L. Ferrero.

New York: G. P. Putnam's Sons, 1909.

See the chapter "Julia and Tiberius" for a popular account of the conflicting personalities of Augustus' daughter Julia and her husband Tiberius. The rises and falls of each in political power are seen as part of the conflict between the old order and the new, symbolized respectively by Tiberius' severity and Julia's loose frivolity.

396. ________. "The Women of the Caesars," [trans. Christian Gauss], Century Magazine, LXXXII (May-October, 1911), 3-14, 225-239, 399-414, 610-623, 651-665, 806-823.

This series of articles in monthly installments reprints in its entirety Ferrero's book of the same title (see below), complete with all the illustrations in the book, and a few more besides. The six chapters appear as follows: May--"Woman and Marriage in Ancient Rome"; June--"Livia and Julia"; July--"The Daughters of Agrippa"; August--"Tiberius and Agrippina"; September--"The Sisters of Caligula and the Marriage of Messalina"; and October--"Agrippina, the Mother of Nero."

397. ________. The Women of the Caesars, trans. Christian Gauss. New York: The Century Co., 1911.

This is a highly readable work written for a popular audience, older now but still one of the more important on the subject. The first chapter gives a useful summary of "Woman and Marriage in Ancient Rome," while following chapters attempt to discover the true characters of the imperial women from the rule of Augustus to the death of Nero. The book is copiously illustrated.

398. Finley, M. I. Aspects of Antiquity: Discoveries and Controversies. New York: Viking Press, 1968.

Printed on pages 129-142 is the article "The Silent Women of Rome," which is exactly the same as that published earlier in Horizon (see the following), but without the illustrations.

399. ________. "The Silent Women of Rome," Horizon, VII (Winter, 1965), 56-64.

The author ponders the silence of Roman women in history. More than in most other civilizations, he says, they remained in the background, producing no great writers, rebels, or spokeswomen. The tight limits of their lives are reviewed, as are the outlets in which some women did release their repressed talents: religion and backstairs political intrigues. This is a grimmer assessment of Roman women's lot than one usually encounters.

400. Flannery, Harry W. "Roman Women and the Vote," Classical Journal, XVI (November, 1920), 103-107.
The recent victory of the women's suffrage movement spurred this article into print. Flannery points out parallel struggles in ancient Rome, in particular the campaign against the Oppian Law and the incident which occurred during the Second Triumvirate, when Hortensia went before the triumvirs and gave an impassioned speech, one of the first known, against "taxation without representation."

401. Förtsch, Barbara. Die Politische Rolle der Frau in der Römischen Republik. Stuttgart: W. Kohlhammer, 1935.

402. Fowler, W. Warde. "On the New Fragment of the So-Called Laudatio Turiae (C.I.L. VI. 1527)," Classical Review, XIX (June, 1905), 261-266.
Based on a detailed examination of the tomb inscription known as the "Laudatio Turiae," particularly of a new fragment then recently discovered, this article concludes that the inscription is indeed the utterance of Q. Lucretius Vespillo upon the death of his wife of forty-one years, Turia. In a time of political upheaval this remarkable woman searched out her parents' murderers and saw to it they were punished, defended her home single-handedly against an attack of ruffians, and saved her husband's life by hiding him during the proscriptions.

403. ________. Social Life at Rome in the Age of Cicero. New York: Macmillan Co., 1933.
Chapter V gives a good general summary of "Marriage and the Roman Lady." Marriage, Fowler makes clear, had nothing to do with love, but was rather a matter of serious familial and civic duty. The consequences of this view were the excesses which some women gave way to in the late Republic. Fowler takes note of the dignified position of the Roman matron, then shows us several women of

Cicero's time who failed to live up to this ideal. He closes with a glowing account of Turia (see above).

404. Frank, Tenney. Aspects of Social Behavior in Ancient Rome. Martin Classical Lectures, Vol. II. Cambridge, Mass.: Harvard University Press, 1932.

Chapter I, "The Roman Family," is really a discussion of the position of women in Rome. After cautioning against too great a reliance on laws (which always lag behind current social realities), the author identifies two opposing forces which determined the status of Roman women: firm patriarchal rule (one of the distinctive social institutions of Rome), and the equally-firm social recognition accorded the matron.

405. Friedländer, Ludwig. Roman Life and Manners Under the Early Empire, trans. Leonard A. Magnus. 4 vols. New York: Barnes & Noble, Inc., 1965.

This book was first published in 1907. In volume 1, Chapter V, "The Position of Women," follows Roman girls from the amusements of their childhood to marriage, their freedom as matrons, and the corrupting influences of spectacles, banquets, and various religious cults. It paints a grim picture of their immorality and frivolous excesses.

406. Gabriel, Mabel M. Livia's Garden Room at Prima Porta. New York: New York University Press, 1955.

This art book treats in detail the superb garden paintings found in the summer villa built outside Rome for Livia sometime around 30 B.C. Black-and-white plates, as well as extensive identification of the birds and trees depicted, accompany the text. "A precious gem which stands alone" among ancient paintings, Livia's garden room reflects the exquisite taste and artistic appreciation for which she was noted.

407. Gardner, Percy. "A New Portrait of Livia," Journal of Roman Studies, XII (1922), 32-34.

A fine portrait bust acquired by the Ashmolean Museum in 1917--certainly the likeness of an imperial lady of Augustus' period--is identified by the author as Livia, the emperor's wife. A brief summary of her life is given, and two plates accompany the article:

one of the Ashmolean bust, the other for comparison of a bust in the Louvre.

408. Gaudemet, Jean. "Le Statut de la Femme dans l'Empire Romain," pp. 191-222 in La Femme. Recueils de la Société Jean Bodin, Vol. XI. Bruxelles: Éditions de la Librairie Encyclopédique, 1959.

This is a good overview of the social and juridical condition of women under the Roman Empire. Noting the strong contrast of their independence and legal capacity with ancient Roman mores, it concentrates especially on the matron's place in the family and her legal rights, particularly in regard to the law of marriage and divorce. Numerous ancient and modern references are noted.

409. Gay, Stewart Irwin. "The Beautiful Queen Zenobia," Transactions and Proceedings of the American Philological Association, LXXI (1940), xxxv-xxxvi.

This is a resume of Gay's paper presented at the annual meeting of the A. P. A. --a biographical picture of Zenobia based on primary and secondary sources. The summary given here praises her beauty and talents and gives a short overview of her career.

410. Giannelli, Giulio. Giulia e Servilia. Donne di Roma Antica, No. 3. Rome: Istituto di Studi Romani, 1945.

This detailed scholarly study in Italian gives the life stories of two more women of ancient Rome: Julia, daughter of Julius Caesar, and Servilia, his influential mistress.

411. Göbl, Robert. Regalianus und Dryantilla: Dokumentation, Münzen, Texte, Epigraphisches. Wien: Köln, Graz, Böhlau, 1970.

This book discusses Sulpicia Dryantilla, wife of Regalianus, the pretender to the imperial throne.

412. Godefroidt, G. "Octavia c. f. Soror Augusti Caesaris: Essai Biographique." Unpublished Doctor's dissertation, Université de Louvain, 1950.

413. Godolphin, Francis Richard Borroum. "A Note on the Marriage of Claudius and Agrippina," Classical

Philology, XXIX (April, 1934), 143-145.

Agrippina the Younger married Emperor Claudius, her uncle. Marriage between such close relatives was not, however, permitted in Roman law until the law was changed for their benefit. Godolphin argues that, as both Claudius and Agrippina had Jewish friends and hence some knowledge of Jewish custom (which allowed such marriages), they bolstered their case with an appeal to Jewish precedent.

414. Grether, Gertrude E. "The Divinity of Women in the Roman Imperial Families, 27 B. C. -235 A. D." Unpublished Doctor's dissertation, Cornell University, 1939.

415. ________. "Livia and the Roman Imperial Cult," American Journal of Philology, LXVII (July, 1946), 222-252.

This is an exhaustive study of the various civil and divine honors accorded to Livia from the early years of Augustus' rule to sometime during the reign of Marcus Aurelius or Commodus, when she was apparently dropped from the imperial cult. Three periods of her public adulation are distinguished: during Augustus' life, after his death, and after her own death.

416. Grimal, Pierre. "La Femme à Rome et dans la Civilisation Romaine," pp. 375-485 in Préhistoire et Antiquité. Vol. I of Histoire Mondiale de la Femme. Paris: Nouveau Librairie de France, 1965.

Grimal discusses in detail the women of archaic Rome, tackling the difficult Etruscans by suggesting they were neither matriarchal nor patriarchal, but truly equal. Next he discusses the lives of women in the Republic and the Empire--their legal position, social and cultural role, political life, economic situation, and intellectual activities. All levels of society are included, from ladies of the imperial house to common slaves. Grimal closes with a short look at Roman women under the impact of Christianity.

417. ________. Love in Ancient Rome, trans. Arthur Train, Jr. New York: Crown Publishers, 1967.

Through his investigation of the Roman attitudes on love and marriage, as revealed in Roman religion, legend, and literature, the author reveals the position of importance held by women in ancient Rome. This is illustrated by the essential view of marriage as a partnership, the gradual loosening of divorce laws, and the recognition of woman's right also to freedom in love. Grimal discusses the powerful political influence of Roman women, too.

418. Gross, Walter Hatto. Iulia Augusta: Untersuchungen zur Grundlegung einer Livia-Ikonographie. Göttingen: Vandenhoeck & Ruprecht, 1962.

This is an iconographic study on the portraiture of the Empress Livia. Gross begins with a comprehensive survey of her likenesses on coins of the imperial mints, on those of provincial Augustan mints, and then on post-Augustan provincial issues. He next examines sculptural reliefs, and finally sculptured portraits in the round. Thirty plates of photographs complete the work.

419. Hadas, Moses. "Vestal Virgins and Runaway Slaves," Classical Weekly, XXIV (February 2, 1931), 108.

This brief note attempts to explain an incident involving runaway slaves after the Battle of Philippi. The Vestal Virgins offered prayers to stem the tide of fugitives, and Hadas speculates that their intervention was appropriate inasmuch as the Vestals may have had power to offer asylum to suppliant slaves if they chose.

420. Hallett, Judith P. "The Role of Women in Roman Elegy: Counter-Cultural Feminism," Arethusa, VI (Spring, 1973), 103-124.

Ms. Hallett looks at the poetry of the amatory elegists and sees in them the protests of a "counter-culture" (much like our own of recent years) against "an inequitable, hypocritical society." Their characterization of their mistresses serves as an example: the women in these poems are appreciated as persons in their own right, exalted and glorified, in direct contrast to contemporary Roman society, which relegated women to a subservient role, regarded them as chattel, and made use of them as "insensate political pawns."

421. Hamilton, Gail. "The Ladies of the Last Caesars," North American Review, CLI (November, 1890), 548-566.

Third and last in a series of rhetorical articles on famous Roman ladies, nearly all of whom the author chooses to see as vile, wicked monsters, this takes up the tale with the death of Tiberius, presenting to us several powerful women of the imperial family to the death of Nero.

422. ________. "Society Women Before Christ," North American Review, CLI (August, 1890), 146-159.

This is an introduction to several highborn ladies of Rome during the age of Caesar and Cicero, their fortunes and misfortunes--especially the politically-motivated divorces which victimized them during that turbulent time.

423. ________. "Society Women of the Time of Christ," North American Review, CLI (September, 1890), 274-288.

This introduces the reader to several important ladies of Augustus' time as the author sees them: sinister Livia, meddlesome Octavia, bloodthirsty Fulvia, and vile Julia. The author's style waxes rhetorical, as in this representative passage: "Ah! what sweet, slow length of golden Roman days might have filled their happy home with sunshine could but Fate have given them to each other who were so near and yet so far!"

424. Hecker, Eugene Arthur. A Short History of Women's Rights from the Days of Augustus to the Present Time: With Special Reference to England and the United States. New York: G. P. Putnam's Sons, 1910.

The first chapter of this book gives in fifty pages a thorough analysis of the rights of women under Roman law, from the time of Augustus in 27 B.C. to Justinian in 527 A.D. Detailed footnotes give complete citations to the legal codes and authors used as sources for the text. Authoritative, and important as a reference work, this book has recently been reprinted.

425. Herrmann, Claudine. Le Rôle Judiciaire et Politique des Femmes sous la République Romaine. Collection Latomus, Vol. 68. Bruxelles: Latomus, 1964.

The author, a doctor of law, reviews the history of the legal and political position of Roman women of the Republic. Although a little too eager to see manifestations of antifeminist persecution and the battle of the sexes in Republican history, Dr. Herrmann's work is well-documented, with an extensive bibliography.

426. Hiesinger, Ulrich S. "Julia Domna: Two Portraits in Bronze," American Journal of Archaeology, LXXIII (January, 1969), 39-44.

This article is on the bronze bust identified as Julia Domna now in the Fogg Art Museum at Harvard. The empress is sympathetically shown as a lovely, rather dreamy, young woman. Comparisons with other representations of her are made, along with discussions of her life and interests. Photographic plates illustrate several of her portraits.

427. Hoffsten, Ruth Bertha. Roman Women of Rank of the Early Empire in Public Life as Portrayed by Dio, Paterculus, Suetonius, and Tacitus. Philadelphia: University of Pennsylvania, 1939.

Here is an excellent dissertation on the social, political, and religious role of noble Roman women from the reigns of Augustus to Nero; specific study is given to the influence of many women of the imperial household. Stress is laid on the large part played by women in public affairs in Rome and throughout the Empire. Uniting in a single slim volume a composite picture of great value, this book is copiously footnoted, with a useful bibliography.

428. Hopkins, M. K. "The Age of Roman Girls at Marriage," Population Studies, XVIII, 3 (1965), 309-327.

After studying ancient literary and epigraphic sources, the author concludes that Roman girls were married before puberty and that, in spite of their youth, their marriages were consummated immediately.

429. Howard, Albert Andrew. "The Institution of the Vestal Virgins at Rome," Overland Monthly, 2nd ser., XVI (August, 1890), 136-149.

This is a clear exposition for the layman of the selection, duties, and privileges of the Vestal Virgins, tracing the history of the institution and its relation to ancient purification rituals and reverence for fire.

430. Iacobacci, Rora F. "Women of Mathematics,"

Arithmetic Teacher, XVII (April, 1970), 316-324. See below.

431. ________. "Women of Mathematics," Mathematics Teacher, LXIII (April, 1970), 329-337.

This special feature, appearing simultaneously in both periodicals, briefly considers the life and work of five women who achieved mathematical distinction. The first sketch summarizes the accomplishments of Hypatia, the first woman mathematician and the only one of importance before the eighteenth century.

432. Johnson, W. H. "The Sister-in-Law of Cicero," Classical Journal, VIII (January, 1913), 160-165.

The marital problems of Cicero's brother Quintus are described here, as revealed in Cicero's own private correspondence. Playing the matchmaker, he had arranged a marriage between his brother and Pomponia, the sister of his lifelong friend, Atticus. Quintus, however, was a hot-tempered fellow, and "evidently Pomponia was irritable and pettish," too. Needless to say, they got along badly together and finally, after some twenty years, were divorced.

433. Johnston, Mary. Roman Life. Glenview, Ill.: Scott, Foresman and Co., 1957.

Profusely illustrated with photographs, this book gives especially fine coverage to Roman women. Most important are the chapters on Roman families, Roman names, clothing of women and girls, Roman religion, and the chapter on "Marriage Customs and Roman Women." This work is a revision of the earlier Private Life of the Romans, by Harold Whetstone Johnston, 1932, which also gave good coverage of marriage customs and the position of women in Rome.

434. ________. "Widows in the First and the Seventeenth Centuries," Classical Weekly, XXV (November 16, 1931), 48.

Wealthy Roman widows of the first century A.D. were constantly bombarded by the assiduous attentions of legacy hunters. Several instances in Roman literature are cited in this short note, and the timelessness of the situation is indicated by a parallel occurrence in seventeenth-century England.

435. Katzoff, Ranon. "Where Was Agrippina Murdered?" Historia, XXII, 1 (1973), 72-78.

The author retells the story of Agrippina's murder, then tackles the problem of exactly where she was when stabbed. He concludes that, after the unsuccessful attempt to drown her at sea, she swam ashore and returned to her villa at Baiae, where she was murdered.

436. Kiefer, Otto. Sexual Life in Ancient Rome, trans. Gilbert and Helen Highet. London: Panther Books, 1969.

Women of course figure prominently in this thorough study of Roman sexual life and customs; chapter I, "Woman in Roman Life," is especially relevant. The author notes the sexual, economic, and political emancipation achieved by women as Rome became more sophisticated and cosmopolitan. With sophistication came women's assertion of their own right to happiness, regarded as degeneracy by those men indoctrinated in the old patriarchal morality.

437. Kornemann, Ernst. Grosse Frauen des Altertums, im Rahmen Zweitausendjährigen Weltgeschehens. Bremen: C. Schünemann, 1958.

This book contains biographies of ancient women; it has been translated into French by G. Welsch under the title, Femmes Illustres de l'Antiquité (Paris: Horizons de France, 1958). Included are Livia, Agrippina the Elder, Julia Domna, Julia Maesa, Julia Mamaea, Zenobia, and Galla Placidia.

438. Le Gall, J. "Métiers de Femmes au Corpus Inscriptionum Latinarum," pp. 123-130 in Mélanges Marcel Durry. Paris: Les Belles Lettres, 1970.

This examination of ancient inscriptions reveals that Roman women engaged not only in humble trades, but that they sometimes had administrative responsibilities as well. Special attention is given to midwives and women doctors.

439. Leon, Ernestine F. "Bobs vs. Knobs in Imperial Rome," Art and Archaeology, XXIV (November, 1927), 170-175.

The changing hair styles of the Roman Empire, from Cleopatra in 50 B.C. to Julia Domna over two centuries later, are displayed as seen in portrait busts of imperial ladies of the time. Ms. Leon takes her subject seriously, a refreshing change from the facetious levity often encountered in male authors.

440. ________. "'Miss Roma'--200 B. C., " The Mentor, XVI (October, 1928), 49-51.

This short, popularized article aims to give "an idea of the appearance of the girl who might have won a beauty contest in Rome in the second century before the Christian era." It is illustrated with mawkish, dated nineteenth-century paintings.

441. ________. "Notes on Caecilia Attica," Classical Bulletin, XXXVIII (January, 1962), 35-36.

Relying largely on the letters of Cicero, Ms. Leon takes a look at the daughter of his closest friend, Atticus. Her life is followed from her birth to her apparently early death. Her daughter Vipsania was the beloved first wife of Emperor Tiberius, and her life is reviewed, also.

442. ________. "Scribonia and Her Daughters," Transactions and Proceedings of the American Philological Association, LXXXII (1951), 168-175.

This article, based on all the scattered references in Roman literature and inscriptions, offers a reconsideration of the character of Scribonia, Octavian's first wife, who is usually dismissed as a nagging, disagreeable person; the author takes a more favorable view of her character. Also reviewed are the lives and personalities of her two daughters--Cornelia by one Cornelius Scipio and Julia by Octavian--who were respectively the most virtuous and most notorious Roman women of their generation.

443. Lilja, Saara. The Roman Elegists' Attitude to Women. Annales Academiae Scientiarum Fennicae, Ser. B, Vol. 135, 1. Helsinki: Suomalainen Tiedeakatemian, 1965.

This is an investigation which aims to give a "synthetical picture" of the attitude towards women expressed by the Roman elegiac poets, in particular Tibullus, Propertius, and Ovid. Attention is also given to the contemporary social background.

444. McCabe, Joseph. The Empresses of Rome. New York: H. Holt and Co., 1911.

In this, one of the basic works on the empresses of both Eastern and Western Empires from Livia to the fall of Rome in 476 A. D., the empresses' careers are reviewed in individual biographical chapters. Well written and eminently readable, the book is not of a scholarly nature, and, unfortunately, there are no footnotes or bibliography to indicate sources. Photographs of busts and coins make this the best single source of portraits of all the empresses.

445. ________. "Hypatia," Critic, XLIII (September, 1903), 267-272.

Hypatia's career is reviewed here largely in order to refute the distorted portrait of her in Charles Kingsley's historical novel, Hypatia. McCabe sees Hypatia as a remarkable exception to the fact that "during the whole of historic time, in almost every civilization..., the growth of woman's mind has been repressed and distorted." He deplores how the Neo-Platonic philosopher, mathematician, and astronomer has become transformed in Kingsley's fictional work into a simple, gullible bluestocking.

446. McDaniel, Walton Brooks. "Bauli the Scene of the Murder of Agrippina," Classical Quarterly, IV (April, 1910), 96-102.

The author attempts a reconstruction of Agrippina the Younger's last hours. His particular concern is with the location of Bauli, where the villa in which she was murdered was located. Bauli, he says, was north, not south, of Baiae, between the Punta dell' Epitafio and the Lucrine Lake.

447. McDermott, William C. "The Sisters of P. Clodius," Phoenix, XXIV (Spring, 1970), 39-47.

The infamous Clodia had two other sisters, one younger and one older. In addition, suggests the author, two earlier sisters had died young. All, following good Roman practice, were named Clodia. This carefully-documented study distinguishes them and elucidates their relationships with their brothers and with Cicero.

448. Macurdy, Grace Harriet. "Julia Berenice," American Journal of Philology, LVI (July, 1935), 246-253.

This article reviews the career of the Jewish princess Berenice, mistress of Emperor Titus and "one of the eminent women of the first century"; her importance in sharing the royal power is stressed. Examination of the accounts of ancient authors reveals brief but vivid glimpses of her character and charm. The story of her alleged incest with her brother Miss Macurdy finds doubtful.

449. ________. Vassal-Queens and Some Contemporary Women in the Roman Empire. Johns Hopkins University Studies in Archaeology, No. 22. Baltimore: Johns Hopkins University Press, 1937.

Miss Macurdy, professor of Greek at Vassar College, here continues where her earlier Hellenistic Queens (number 258) left off. She gives an account of women belonging to the royal houses subject to Rome in the first century A.D., as well as Roman women of the imperial family at the same time. This is a scholarly work with a valuable bibliography, a reliable source of information on many women neglected in most histories.

450. Maiuri, Amedeo. "The Statue of Livia from the Villa of the Mysteries," trans. Arthur Stanley Riggs, Art and Archaeology, XXXIII (July-August, 1932), 170-174, 222.

The author narrates how a beautiful marble statue of a lady in the garb and pose of a priestess was discovered still standing, undamaged, at Pompeii. It is identified as "one of the most beautiful and characteristic of all the portraits of Livia," the woman who "divided with Augustus the heavy responsibilities of ordering the destinies of Rome."

451. Malcovati, Enrica. Clodia, Fulvia, Marzia, Terenzia. Donne di Roma Antica, No. 1. Rome: Istituto di Studi Romani, 1944.

This is a study in Italian of the lives of four Roman women who played important roles during the "tragica agonia della repubblica." It is well documented, with citations to the original sources.

452. Maniet, A. "Pline le Jeune et Calpurnia: Etude Sémantique et Psychologique," L'Antiquité Classique, XXXV (1966), 149-185.

The author discusses the happy and long-lasting marriage of Calpurnia to Pliny the Younger, which had a solid foundation in their common tastes and personalities.

453. Marshall, F. H. "The Position of Women," pp. 184-190 in A Companion to Latin Studies, ed. John Edwin Sandys. 3rd ed. New York: Hafner Publishing Co., 1963.

This useful summary of the condition of Roman women analyzes their position under the Republic and the Empire. Topics discussed include women's legal condition, women in literature, women and religion, the amusements and occupations of women, and their political influence. A few original sources are cited.

454. Mattingly, Harold. "The Consecration of Faustina the Elder and Her Daughter," Harvard Theological Review, XLI (April, 1948), 147-151.

Taking as a starting point the unusually numerous coins minted in honor of these two "revered ladies in eternity," and the profusion of honors heaped upon them, Mattingly sees in their consecration an expression of how deeply their husbands loved them. Consecration of women was common enough, but Antoninus Pius and Marcus Aurelius did not allow the worship of the two Faustinas to sink into oblivion after the inaugural flurry. The persistence of their devotion suggests that the "venomous gossip" surrounding the two women was groundless.

455. Mazzarino, Santo. Serena e le Due Eudossie. Donne di Roma Antica, No. 7. Rome: Istituto di Studi Romani, 1946.

This monograph deals with three women of the late Roman Empire in the East, their careers and achievements. Serena was the ambitious wife of the powerful general, Stilicho, and the two Eudocias were later empresses who ruled the Eastern Empire, in reality if not in name.

456. Mills, Dorothy. The Book of the Ancient Romans. New York: G. P. Putnam's Sons, 1937.

Intended as an introduction, for high school age readers and up, to the history and civilization of Rome, this book contains a good chapter on "The Roman Lady." Quoting ancient authors in its discussion, it describes how Roman women were held in greater honor than those of any other nation in the ancient world. Long discussion of the sumptuary law during the Punic War is followed by a discussion of the marriage ceremony.

457. Mireaux, Emile. La Reine Bérénice. Paris: Albin Michel, 1951.

This is a biography of Julia Berenice, daughter of Herod Agrippa and mistress of Emperor Titus. It closes with a chapter on Berenice's treatment in French literature.

458. Mohler, S. L. "Feminism in the Corpus Inscriptionum Latinarum," Classical Weekly, XXV (February 15, 1932), 113-117.

From the large body of surviving Latin inscriptions a picture is here drawn of the part women played in the public life of communities outside of Rome. Women freely attended the games and public meals, but their participation was not limited to this passive role. A Roman secured the good opinion of his fellow-citizens not by amassing great wealth, but by giving it away, making contributions to his community. Women had almost equal opportunities to become public benefactors as men, especially in their positions as priestesses, and many examples are given here of female generosity.

459. Mommsen, Theodor. "Porcia," Hermes, XV (1880), 99-102.

Mommsen contends that Porcia (Brutus' wife) was the sister, not the daughter, of Cato.

460. Motto, Anna Lydia. "Seneca on Women's Liberation," Classical World, LXV (January, 1972), 155-157.

The author reviews Seneca's views of women. His attitudes were patriarchal, and he condemned their wickedness in his own degenerate time. Yet, he believed women were equal in abilities.

461. Mullens, H. G. "The Women of the Caesars," Greece and Rome, XI (February, 1942), 59-67.

Mullens points out that among the Julio-Claudians and the Antonines the continuation of the dynasty and succession to the throne depended upon the women of the line. Thus, they attained official positions of extraordinary power and received the title Augusta, which had connotations of divinity and imperial authority. The ultimate expression of this was Agrippina's suggestion that she marry her son Nero, by which action her power to dispose of the throne and legitimize his position would be made manifest.

462. Nagl, Maria Assunta. Galla Placidia. Studien zur Geschichte und Kultur des Altertums, Bd. 2, Hft. 3. Paderborn: F. Schöningh, 1908.

463. Noailles, Pierre. "Le Procès de Virginie," Revue des Etudes Latines, XX (1942), 106-138.
This is a lengthy legal interpretation of the legendary trial of Virginia and all the legalistic ploys used, complete with Latin terminology.

464. Oliver, James H. "Livia as Artemis Boulaia at Athens," Classical Philology, LX (July, 1965), 179.
This short, learned note points out that Livia was assimilated to the goddess Artemis Boulaia in an Athenian inscription.

465. ________. "Lollia Paulina, Memmius Regulus and Caligula," Hesperia, XXXV (April-June, 1966), 150-153.
Lollia Paulina was married to the imperial legate in Greece, Memmius Regulus, in a Greek form of marriage, but when Emperor Caligula capriciously claimed the bride for himself, Memmius had no choice but to comply. Because his Greek form did not have the legal weight of a Roman marriage, Oliver says, Memmius had no legitimate grievance; in fact, he had cautiously chosen this course in order to be able to accommodate Caligula if it proved necessary.

466. Olson, H. "The Five Julias of the Severan Emperors," The Voice of the Turtle, IV (1965), 197.
This article contains coin portraits of Julia Domna, Julia Maesa, Julia Mamaea, Julia Soaemias, and the lesser-known Julia Cornelia Paula.

467. Oost, Stewart Irvin. "Galla Placidia and the Law," Classical Philology, LXIII (April, 1968), 114-121.
Galla Placidia was taken captive by, and later married, Athaulf, King of the Visigoths. Thereafter, he held a great respect for the Roman Empire and its rule of law. Oost suggests that Placidia, who had "firm views both on the position of the law in the state as well as the proper relation of the ruler to the law," was responsible for this change. Transforming a barbarian king bent on destroying the Empire into a philo-Roman was indeed the greatest service Galla Placidia could render to her fatherland.

468. ________. Galla Placidia Augusta: A Biographical Essay. Chicago: University of Chicago Press, 1968.

This is the only major account in English of the life of Galla Placidia. Based on careful study of the original sources, and copiously footnoted, the book combines scholarship with readable prose. Oost places Galla's career against the context of her time, the barbarians, the Roman Empire, and the imperial dynasty of her family, occasionally filling in the sketchy details of history with hypothetical speculations. A lengthy bibliography of secondary works cited is included.

469. ________. "Some Problems in the History of Galla Placidia," Classical Philology, LX (January, 1965), 1-10.

Here are three notes of interest mostly to the professional scholar. The first attempts to figure out just when Galla Placidia was born (probably in 388 A. D.), the second offers an interpretation of a poem by Merobaudes in which Galla Placidia figures, and the third inquires into where her nephew, her infant son Theodosius, and she herself were buried (in Rome, not at Ravenna in the well-known "Mausoleum of Galla Placidia").

470. Palmerlee, Grace. "The Coiffure of Roman Women as Shown on Portrait Busts and Statues," Records of the Past, IX (May-June, 1910), 166-176.

Awkwardly written, this article describes in detail the hair styles of Roman women from the late Republic to the third century A. D. The author classifies them into eight types: the late Republic, early Empire, Flavian, Matidia, Faustina, Lucilla, Julia Domna, and third century types. Lastly, there is the "fixed," unchanging style of the Vestal Virgins. Numerous photographs of Roman statues and coins illustrate the styles explained in the text.

471. Paratore, Ettore. "Un Evento Clamoroso nella Roma di Millenovecento Anni Fa," Studi Romani, VII (September-October, 1959), 497-510.

Paratore believes that the murder of Agrippina the Younger marked the beginning of the decline of the Roman Empire. In this article he discusses that act and the circumstances which led up to it.

472. ________. Plotina, Sabina e le Due Faustine. Donne di Roma Antica, No. 2. Rome: Istituto di Studi Romani, 1945.

The lives of four empresses of Rome--Plotina, Sabina, Faustina the Elder, and Faustina the Younger--are given in this twenty-five page booklet, a detailed account of what is known about them.

473. Paris, Pierre. Quatenus Feminae Res Publicas in Asia Minore, Romanis Imperantibus, Attigerint. Paris: E. Thorin, 1891.

This thesis examines the extent to which women handled public affairs in the Asian provinces of the Roman Empire.

474. Pastorino, A. "La Sempronia della Congiura di Catilina," Giornale Italiano di Filologia, III (1950), 358-363.

Pastorino discusses the Sempronia who was part of Catiline's conspiracy, noting changes of opinion about her in Cicero and Sallust.

475. Pfister, Kurt. Die Frauen der Cäsaren. Berlin: A. Nauck, 1951.

476. Pichon, René. "Le Rôle Religieux des Femmes dans l'Ancienne Rome," Annales du Musée Guimet, Bibliothèque de Vulgarisation, XXXIX (1912), 77-135.

Pichon offers an extensive analysis of woman's role in ancient Roman religion. In the early period of the Republic women were important, but never equal to men or independent of them, in religious observances. The foreign cults which were introduced into Rome later, though, raised women to an equal position with male worshippers and gave them an equal sacerdotal role as well.

477. Pierret, Paul. Le Senatusconsulte Velléien: Etude sur l'Incapacité Civile de la Femme à Rome. Thuillies: Les Editions Ramgal, 1947.

After a preliminary look at the text, date, etc. of the Vellaean senatus consultum, Dr. Pierret briefly reviews the legal position of Roman women, then launches into a legal examination of the decree--its antecedents, how it established the legal incapacity of women, and how Justinian's legal reforms changed it.

478. Pink, K. "Magnia Urbica," Numismatische Zeitschrift, LXXIX (1961), 5-9.

An examination of Magnia Urbica's coins throws some light on her life, her husband and son, and her honorary titles as "Augusta" and "Mater Castrorum."

479. Piper, Linda J. "Livy's Portrayal of Early Roman Women," Classical Bulletin, XLVIII (December, 1971), 26-28.

480. Polaschek, Karin. Studien zur Ikonographie der Antonia Minor. Roma: "L'Erma" di Bretschneider, 1973.

This is a scholarly study of the various representations of Antonia Minor in ancient art, classified by stylistic types. At the back of the book, twenty-three pages of clear photographic plates illustrate several of her portrait busts.

481. Putnam, Emily James. "The Roman Lady," Atlantic Monthly, CV (June, 1910), 758-794.

Ms. Putnam gives us a look at the strong-willed, independent Roman woman of the upper classes, noting her individual importance as a person in her own right. A slightly abridged version of the third chapter of her book, The Lady (number 187), this article was also published in Contemporary Review, XCVII (May, 1910), 555-567.

482. Rankin, H. D. "Clodia II," L'Antiquité Classique, XXXVIII, 2 (1969), 501-506.

Rankin finds it "difficult to doubt" that the Lesbia of Catullus' poetry was Clodia, the same woman attacked by Cicero in his "Pro Caelio." A look at the characterizations of her by Cicero, Catullus, and others indicates that they were clearly talking about the same woman.

483. Raubitschek, Antony E. "Octavia's Deification at Athens," Transactions of the American Philological Association, LXXVII (1946), 146-150.

This interpretation of ancient inscriptions and a passage in Seneca's Suasoriae (i. 6-7), suggests that Octavia, while in Athens as Mark Antony's wife, was identified with their goddess Athena Polias and received divine honors.

484. Richeson, A. W. "Hypatia of Alexandria," National Mathematics Magazine, XV (November, 1940), 74-82.

485. Richmond, I. A. "Queen Cartimandua," Journal of Roman Studies, XLIV (1954), 43-52.

This is the most important article (in fact, the only article) yet written on Cartimandua, the powerful queen of the Brigantes in northern Britain. It investigates in depth her realm, her history, and how she supported Roman rule and quashed local opposition to it.

486. Rist, J. M. "Hypatia," Phoenix, XIX (1965), 214-225.

487. Roberts, Martha Lizzie. "Status of Woman in Roman Law." Unpublished Doctor's dissertation, Boston University, 1896.

488. Rogers, Robert Samuel. "The Conspiracy of Agrippina," Transactions and Proceedings of the American Philological Association, LXII (1931), 141-168.

Agrippina the Elder, daughter of Julia Major, was a direct descendant of Augustus. The same can not be said of his successor, Tiberius. Although the portrait left us by Tacitus is favorable, Rogers presents her instead as an ambitious and imperious woman, stubborn, proud, and indomitable of spirit. Various conspiracies against Tiberius surfaced following his accession to the throne, and Rogers connects them all to a faction for Agrippina. He is certain that she plotted against Tiberius, and he reconstructs step by step the history of the plot until her suicide on October 18, 33 A. D.

489. ________. "The Deaths of Julia and Gracchus, A. D. 14," Transactions and Proceedings of the American Philological Association, XCVIII (1967), 383-390.

Reviewing the circumstances of Julia Major's exile and death, and the political implications of whether or not she was murdered, Rogers concludes that she died a natural death and that stories to the contrary are merely rumors created in the interests of Tiberius' political enemies.

490. ________. "Fulvia Paulina C. Sentii Saturnini," American Journal of Philology, LIII (July, 1932), 252-256.

In the year 19 A. D. several investigations and trials disclosed scandalous outrages against Roman morality. Two cases involved the wife of Saturninus--called Fulvia in one case and Paulina in the other. Rogers proposes that both cases involve one and the same woman (Fulvia Paulina being her real name), a woman "of great dignity" who was unwittingly involved in some flagrant abuses of the acceptable practice of temple prostitution.

491. ________. "An Incident of the Opposition to Tiberius," Classical Journal, XLVII (December, 1951), 114-115.

When a Roman died, it was customary for him to remember in his will the outstanding public figures of his day. When Junia, the sister of Brutus and widow of Cassius, died, she expressed her opposition to Emperor Tiberius by leaving him no such legacy. Moreover, in her funeral procession the images of her brother and husband (conspirators against Tiberius' ancestor-by-adoption, Julius Caesar) were conspicuous in their absence, an omission which served as another subtle bit of anti-Tiberian propaganda.

492. Rose, Herbert J. "De Virginibus Vestalibus," Mnemosyne, 2nd ser., LIV, 4 (1926), 440-448.

Rose, writing in Latin, discusses the importance of the chastity of the Vestal Virgins in the proper execution of their religious functions. Chosen between the ages of six and ten, they were looked on more as daughters than as matrons, because it was felt that the prayers of girls would be more pleasing to Vesta.

493. ________. "Iterum de Virginibus Vestalibus," Mnemosyne, 2nd ser., LVI, 1 (1928), 79-80.

Rose continues his argument (see above) that the Vestal Virgins' role was that of daughters, not matrons. He brings forth a passage from Plutarch which states that matrons were forbidden to bake or pound grain; instead, unmarried daughters performed these tasks. Vestals, however, did bake and crush grain for ceremonial use, a fact which Rose feels confirms his theory that their role was a filial one. Like the previous article, this is written in Latin.

494. ________. "Mother-Right in Ancient Italy," Folk-Lore, XXXI (June, 1920), 93-108.

Rose's search is for the existence in ancient Italy of mother-right: the system "by which inheritance of name or property, position with regard to family or clan, in fact all that we express by the surname and its associations, come through the mother and not the father." Excepting, of course, the matrilineal Etruscans, Rose finds among the Italians "a system of father-right in its most rigid form." Clearly, the Romans were patrilineal in historical times, and as for remotest antiquity, Rose's examination of the evidence offers no reason to think it was ever otherwise.

495. Rowland, Robert G. "Sallust's Wife," *Classical World*, LXII (December, 1968), 134.

Tradition asserts that after Cicero divorced her, Terentia married Sallust. Cicero then took another wife, Publilia. Various men are said to have married "Cicero's wife." This article attempts to sort out the conflicting testimony and figure out just who married which one.

496. Rumpf, Andreas. *Antonia Augusta*. Berlin: W. de Gruyter, 1941.

This is about Antonia Minor.

497. Schilling, Robert. "Vestales et Vierges Chrétiennes dans la Rome Antique," *Revue des Sciences Religieuses*, XXXV (April, 1961), 113-129.

Schilling notes the essential differences between the Vestal Virgins and early Christian virgins--most notably that the Christian was pledged for life, the Vestal for only thirty years, after which she could marry if she chose. These differences revolve around the fact that the Vestal was pledged only to the service of an earthly city, but the Christian to a city of God.

498. Schmidt, Otto Eduard. *Cicero und Terentia*. Leipzig: B. G. Teubner, 1898.

499. Schrek, D. J. E. "Hypatia van Alexandrie," *Euclides*, XXI (1945-46), 164-173.

500. Scott, M. A. "The Rebellion of Boudicca: The Burnt Layer and the Narrative of Tacitus," *Pegasus*, VIII (1967), 12-14.

This article discusses especially our sources of information on Boudicca's rebellion. Tacitus' account, though lacking somewhat in clarity of detail, is essential to fill in the gaps left by the remains of archaeology.

501. Serviez, Jacques Roergas de. Lives of the Roman Empresses: The History of the Lives and Secret Intrigues of the Wives, Sisters and Mothers of the Caesars. New York: Wm. H. Wise & Co., 1935.

This is a new edition (translator unspecified) of a book first published in Paris in 1718 under the title Les Femmes des Douze Premiers Césars. It is a treasure trove of information on all the Roman empresses from Calpurnia, wife of Julius Caesar, to Constantia, sister of Constantine; an individual chapter is devoted to each woman. Popular in approach, aiming to entertain, it unfortunately suffers from inaccuracies, obsolete platitudes, and insipid illustrations whose goal is "an intimate insight into the sensuous luxury of ancient Rome."

502. Singer, Mary White. "Octavia Minor, Sister of Augustus: An Historical and Biographical Study." Unpublished Doctor's dissertation, Duke University, 1945.

503. ________. "Octavia's Mediation at Tarentum," Classical Journal, XLIII (December, 1947), 173-177.

After describing in detail the negotiations between Octavian and Mark Antony in 37 B.C., Dr. Singer states that Octavia's role as mediator has been exaggerated. Although she may have had some influence, "it could scarcely have been a basic or even a decisive factor in the treaty."

504. ________. "The Problem of Octavia Minor and Octavia Maior," Transactions and Proceedings of the American Philological Association, LXXIX (1948), 268-274.

Caesar Augustus had two sisters named Octavia: a half sister, Octavia Maior, and a full sister, Octavia Minor. The problem is to determine which one was married to Mark Antony. Investigation of the confusing testimony of ancient sources leads Dr. Singer to conclude that Octavia Minor, the younger of the two, was the famous Octavia, Antony's wife.

505. Sirago, Vito Antonio. Galla Placidia e la Trasformazione Politica dell' Occidente. Recueil de Travaux d'Histoire et de Philologie, Ser. 4, No. 25. Louvain: Bibliothèque de l'Université Catholique, 1961.

A history of the Western Empire from 408-455 A.D., this book emphasizes the conflict between the "center" (the government at Ravenna) and the "periphery" (barbarian invaders and Catholic bishops). Galla Placidia is prominent as a key figure in the "center," who helped initiate the "political transformation of the West." Sirago suggests that her main achievement was the Romanization of the Visigoths, and that she thus deserves to be known as the first great educator of the barbarians.

506. Smallwood, E. Mary. "The Alleged Jewish Tendencies of Poppaea Sabina," Journal of Theological Studies, new ser., X (October, 1959), 329-335.

Miss Smallwood denies that Poppaea Sabina, Nero's wife, felt any special sympathy for the Jewish religion. As she puts it, "A woman of Poppaea's ambition, who sought to advance her own position by promiscuity, and who did not shrink from instigating the murders of Agrippina and Octavia in order that she might become empress herself and is not recorded as having shown any remorse for her deeds afterwards, would hardly have been attracted by any religion which expressly forbade murder and adultery."

507. Smethurst, S. E. "Women in Livy's History," Greece and Rome, XIX (June, 1950), 80-87.

Women in Livy's history of Rome generally are lifeless puppets without individuality, incapable of positive action, or else downright wicked. This summary makes clear that Livy plays down their importance in his history largely because his interest is in masculine deeds and virtues.

508. Spence, Lewis. Boadicea, Warrior Queen of the Britons. London: Robert Hale, Ltd., 1937.

509. Stadelmann, Heinrich. Messalina: A Picture of Life in Imperial Rome, trans. H. F. Angold. New York: E. P. Dutton & Co., 1930.

This biography of the notorious wife of Emperor Claudius, relating her career to the history and social life of her times, offers a particularly lurid account of her debauchery presented against "a background of bacchanalian orgies, mysterious gardens and political intrigue."

510. Sullivan, Philip B. "A Note on the Flavian Accession," Classical Journal, XLIX (November, 1953), 67-70, 78.

Though the evidence is admittedly inconclusive, Sullivan concludes from it that Berenice, the beautiful, Hellenized Jewish princess, was a prime mover in the conspiracy which placed Vespasian and his Flavian dynasty on the imperial throne.

511. Teufer, Johannes. Zur Geschichte der Frauenemanzipation im Alten Rom: Eine Studie zu Livius 34, 1-8. Leipzig: B. G. Teubner, 1913.

512. Townend, G. B. "The Trial of Aemilia Lepida in A.D. 20," Latomus, XXI (July-September, 1962), 484-493.

Aemilia Lepida's trial for adultery is here discussed, and the contradictory accounts of Suetonius and Tacitus are analyzed. She was found guilty and, because she was convicted of trying to foist another man's child onto her husband, his estate went not to her but to Emperor Tiberius. It was alleged at the time that the emperor in his avarice engineered the whole trial for his own enrichment, and this allegation is considered, also.

513. Toynbee, Jocelyn. "The Villa Item and a Bride's Ordeal," Journal of Roman Studies, XIX (1929), 67-88.

This ingenious, if unconvincing, article argues that the frescoes of the Villa of the Mysteries outside Pompeii represent Dionysiac initiation rites in which a bride suffered a pre-nuptial ritual flagellation in order to stimulate the procreative powers and promote fertility.

514. Treggiari, Susan. "Libertine Ladies," Classical World, LXIV (February, 1971), 196-198.

This is a short discussion of Roman "libertinae," or freedwomen. The author's purpose is to clear up several misconceptions about these ex-slaves, particularly that they were unable to marry. Although it is true that many did become prostitutes, or high-class mistresses, they could and did marry quite legally.

515. Tucker, T. G. *Life in the Roman World of Nero and St. Paul*. New York: Macmillan Co., 1911.
This popular work on Roman life during the age of Nero gives in Chapter XVI a look at Roman women at that time: how they were married, the matron's freedom, and a glance at their dress and personal adornment.

516. Van Buren, A. W. "Pompeii--Nero--Poppaea," pp. 970-974 in *Studies Presented to David Moore Robinson, Volume II*, ed. George E. Mylonas and Doris Raymond. Saint Louis, Mo.: Washington University, 1953.
The author looks at Pompeian graffiti, in particular a couplet praising her beauty, to deduce that Poppaea was probably a well-known figure in Pompeii, where she was highly honored.

517. Van Deman, Esther Boise. "The Cult of Vesta Publica and the Vestal Virgins." Unpublished Doctor's dissertation, University of Chicago, 1898.

518. Vaughan, Agnes Carr. *Zenobia of Palmyra*. Garden City, N.Y.: Doubleday & Co., 1967.
This is a fine, thoroughly readable work aimed at the general reader as well as the scholar. After providing background on the history of Palmyra, it launches into the reign of Zenobia from her declaration of independence from Rome to her battles with, and ultimate defeat by, Emperor Aurelian. Controversies and gaps in the historical sources are acknowledged, in which cases the author provides her own surmises as to what may have happened.

519. Villers, Robert. "Le Statut de la Femme à Rome jusqu'à la Fin de la République," pp. 177-189 in *La Femme*. Recueils de la Société Jean Bodin, Vol. XI. Bruxelles: Editions de la Librairie Encyclopédique, 1959.
This is a short summary of the stable, subordinate position of women under Roman law, and of their gradual independence from certain restrictions in the later years of the Republic.

520. Waldhauer, Oscar. "A Note on Another Portrait-Head of Livia," *Journal of Roman Studies*, XIII (1923), 190.

This is a brief discussion, prompted by Gardner's earlier article (number 407), of another good portrait bust of the Empress Livia, this time in the Hermitage Museum. A plate showing the bust from the front and in profile is appended at the back of the journal.

521. Wedeck, Harry E. "Synonyms for Meretrix," *Classical Weekly*, XXXVII (January 3, 1944), 116-117.

This little disquisition on the numerous names for prostitutes among the Romans reveals the various types plying their trade then--the officially-recognized "lupae," the musicians and kept women of the upper classes, and the "prostibulae" who served the lower masses. The Romans had quite an extensive vocabulary to choose from, including such colorful names as the "alicaria," who frequented the spelt mills, the "noctuvigila," or "night hag," and the "quadrantaria," whose favors were very cheap.

522. Wegner, Max. *Hadrian, Plotina, Marciana, Matidia, Sabina*. Berlin: Mann, 1956.

523. Weil, Bruno. *Clodia: Roms Grosse Dame und Kurtisane*. Zürich: W. Classen, [1960].

524. Wieand, Helen E. "Position of Women in the Late Roman Republic," *Classical Journal*, XII (March, 1917), 378-392; (April, 1917), 423-437.

Ms. Wieand pictures the position of women in the turbulent period when the Roman Republic was coming to an end. She indicates the paradox of the situation in which "the Roman matron was at once honored and subordinated; she was thoroughly respected and yet granted almost no legal rights." After a general discussion of the forms of Roman marriage, and other legal and social determinants of woman's status, the article abandons generalities and looks at individuals, both virtuous and otherwise, who influenced the course of Republican history.

525. Wiggers, Heinz Bernhard. *Caracalla, Geta, Plautilla*; bound with Max Wegner, *Macrinus bis Balbinus*. West Berlin: Gebrüder Mann, 1971.

This volume is devoted to the portraiture of the Roman emperors and their wives from Caracalla to Balbinus. Among the women included are Plautilla, Julia Maesa, Julia Soaemias, the three wives of Elagabalus, Julia Mamaea, Orbiana, and Paulina. A general discussion of their lives and portraiture precedes a more detailed description of each individual work. At the back of the book over seventy-five photographic plates reproduce many of the busts and coins under discussion.

526. Wild, Payson S. "Two Julias," *Classical Journal*, XIII (October, 1917), 14-24.

This article offers a brief retelling of the "reigns" of Julia Domna and Julia Mamaea, for the author feels that *they* really ran the Empire, not their incompetent sons. He admires them both and credits them with whatever worthy actions were performed during their sons' reigns.

527. Williams, Mary Gilmore. "De Julia Domna." Unpublished Doctor's dissertation, University of Michigan, 1897.

528. ________. "Studies in the Lives of Roman Empresses, I: Julia Domna," *American Journal of Archaeology*, VI, 3 (1902), 259-305.

This is a thorough, scholarly study, in which the casual, Latin-less reader may feel lost. It investigates the obscure daughter of a Syrian priest, Julia Domna, who became empress by marrying Septimius Severus and was accorded unprecedented titles and honor, and whose son Caracalla exalted her so highly that she became the actual administrative head of the Empire. The article relies strongly on the evidence of ancient inscriptions.

529. ________. "Studies in the Lives of Roman Empresses, II: Julia Mamaea," pp. 67-100 in *Roman Historical Sources and Institutions*, ed. Henry A. Sanders. New York: Johnson Reprint Corp., 1967.

This is a careful study which combines the scanty evidence of literary sources, coins, and inscriptions to determine Julia Mamaea's part in the administration of the Roman Empire. As regent for her son Alexander Severus, who was completely under her influence, she wielded great power. The course of her government is followed from her accession to power to her death at the hands of disloyal centurions. This is a reprint of the 1904 original.

530. Willrich, Hugo. Livia. Leipzig: B. G. Teubner, 1911.

531. Wiseman, T. P. "The Mother of Livia Augusta," Historia, XIV (July, 1965), 333-334.

This short note suggests that, despite the statement of Suetonius, Livia's mother was not Aufidia of Fundi, but rather a woman named Alfidia, perhaps from Marruvium.

532. Wolf, Stephan. Hypatia, die Philosophin von Alexandrien: Ihr Leben, Wirken und Lebensende nach den Quellenschriften Dargestellt. Wien: Hölder, 1879.

533. Worsfold, Sir Thomas Cato. The History of the Vestal Virgins of Rome. London: Rider & Co., 1934.

In this exhaustive history of the Vestal Virgins from their origin in 715 B.C. to their abolition in 394 A.D., Worsfold explains the religious duties of the Vestals, as well as their civil duties, privileges, dress, and discipline. He then describes the temples and other monuments associated with the Vestals. This work relies heavily on ancient authors and archaeological remains and is illustrated with plates of the Vestals and their haunts.

534. Wright, William. An Account of Palmyra and Zenobia, with Travels and Adventures in Bashan and the Desert. New York: Thomas Nelson and Sons, 1895.

Written while the author was traveling in Syria and Persia and was inspired by his surroundings, this book for the armchair traveler gives an account of Zenobia's life. Numerous illustrations of Palmyra and surroundings illustrate the narrative.

IV

INDEXES

ABBREVIATIONS USED IN INDEXES

b.	--	born
c.	--	circa
cent.	--	century
d.	--	died
fl.	--	flourished
m.	--	married

INDEX OF WOMEN IN ANTIQUITY

NOTE: Numbers in parentheses refer to the identifying numbers of works in the text.

AEMILIA LEPIDA (fl. 2-20 A. D.), divorced wife of P. Quirinius who was tried and convicted for adultery: (512).

AGRIPPINA THE ELDER (c. 14 B. C. -33 A. D.), wife of Germanicus, daughter of Marcus Agrippa and Julia Major, banished by Tiberius: (367, 396, 397, 488).

AGRIPPINA THE YOUNGER (c. 15-59 A. D.), daughter of the above, wife of Emperor Claudius, mother of Nero: (139, 140, 169, 332, 343, 356, 382, 387, 396, 397, 413, 435, 446, 471).

AMAZONS: (164, 169, 193, 198, 204, 245, 286, 291, 299, 311, 314).

ANTONIA MINOR (36 B. C. -37 A. D.), daughter of Mark Antony and Octavia, wife of Drusus, mother of Germanicus, Livilla, and Claudius: (396, 397, 480, 496).

ANYTE OF TEGEA (fl. 290 B. C.), Arcadian poetess, wrote sepulchral epigrams: (26, 28, 44, 45, 53, 55, 65, 67, 68).

ASPASIA (470-410 B. C.), prominent Athenian hetaera and mistress of Pericles, originally from Miletus: (195, 216, 217, 231, 267, 310).

ASPASIA OF PHOCAEA (c. 400 B. C.), Greek courtesan and beauty, mistress of Artaxerxes II, King of Persia, and his brother, Cyrus the Younger: (228).

AURELIA (d. 54 B. C.), mother of Julius Caesar: (385).

BERENICE, JULIA (28-c. 79 A. D.), Queen of Chalcis, daughter of Agrippa I, mistress of Emperor Titus: (377, 448, 457, 510).

BOADICEA [BOUDICCA] (d. 62 A. D.), British queen of the Iceni, rebelled against Rome and sacked London: (195, 333, 360, 390, 391, 500, 508).

CAECILIA ATTICA (51 B. C. -c. 30 B. C.), daughter of Atticus, wife of Agrippa: (441).

CAERELLIA (fl. c. 45 B. C.), wealthy friend of Cicero: (336).

CALPURNIA (fl. 59-44 B. C.), fourth wife of Julius Caesar: (385).

CALPURNIA (fl. c. 110 A. D.), third wife of Pliny the Younger: (131, 452).

CARTIMANDUA (d. 57 A. D.), queen of the Brigantes in Britain, cooperated with the Romans: (485).

CHARIXENA (fl. 7th or 6th cent. B. C.), Grecian poet, none of whose work is now extant: (42).

CLEA (c. 110 A. D.), priestess at Delphi, friend of Plutarch: (132, 208, 246).

CLEOBULINE (fl. 570 B. C.), Greek poetess noted for her enigmatic riddles in verse: (40, 67, 68).

CLEOPATRA (d. 308 B. C.), sister of Alexander the Great: (261).

CLODIA (fl. 59 B. C.), profligate woman of the late Roman Republic, Catullus' "Lesbia": (104, 105, 388, 447, 451, 482, 523).

CORINNA (fl. 5th cent. B. C.), Greek lyric poetess from Boeotia: (28, 30, 31, 35, 39, 42, 46, 47, 50, 53, 54, 58-60, 63, 66).

CORNELIA (fl. 175-143 B. C.), daughter of Scipio Africanus, mother of the Gracchi: (74, 79, 82, 85, 375).

CORNELIA (b. 40's B. C.), first daughter of Scribonia before she married Augustus, wife of Aemilius Paullus, a virtuous matron: (442).

COSSUTIA (fl. 85 B. C.), first woman to whom Julius Caesar was engaged, and perhaps married: (384, 385).

CRATESIPOLIS (fl. 315-308 B. C.), queen of several Peloponnesian cities, commanded a powerful army of mercenaries: (260).

DIOTIMA (fl. 468 B. C.), learned woman from Mantinea, perhaps a priestess, who taught Socrates the philosophy of love: (127, 128, 130, 233, 234, 266, 270).

DOMITIA LONGINA (fl. 70 A. D.), wife of Emperor Domitian: (379).

DOMITIA LUCILLA (d. 155 A. D.), mother of Marcus Aurelius: (363).

DOMITILLA (d. after 51 A. D.), mother of Domitian and Titus, wife of Vespasian: (379).

DRUSILLA, JULIA (c. 16-38 A. D.), daughter of Agrippina the Elder, sister of Caligula: (396, 397).

DRYANTILLA, SULPICIA -- see Sulpicia Dryantilla.

DYNAMIS (c. 63 B. C. -7 A. D.), Queen of Bosporus: (290).

ERINNA (fl. 4th cent. B. C.), Greek poetess of Telos, wrote "The Distaff," died at 19: (23, 32, 33, 35, 36, 38, 41, 43-45, 49, 52, 53, 55, 56, 63, 67, 68).

EUDOCIA ATHENAIS (393-460 A. D.), wife of the eastern emperor Theodosius II, wrote poetry: (455).

EUDOXIA (d. 404 A. D.), Roman empress, wife of Arcadius: (455).

EURYDICE (fl. 337-317 B. C.), queen of Macedonia, mother of Philip II and grandmother of Alexander the Great: (261).

FALCONIA, PROBA VALERIA -- see Proba, Anicia Faltonia.

FAUSTINA, ANNIA (m. 221 A. D.), third wife of Emperor Elagabalus: (525).

FAUSTINA THE ELDER (c. 104-141 A. D.), wife of Emperor Antoninus Pius: (363, 454, 472).

FAUSTINA THE YOUNGER (c. 130-175 A. D.), daughter of the above, wife of Marcus Aurelius: (454, 472).

FLAVIA CLEA -- see Clea.

FULVIA (d. 40 B. C.), wife of Mark Antony, active in the revolt against Octavian which caused the Perusine War: (340, 348, 451).

FULVIA PAULINA (fl. 19 A. D.), wife of Saturninus: (490).

GALLA PLACIDIA (c. 388-450 A. D.), Roman empress, daughter of Theodosius I, mother of Valentinian III: (462, 467-469, 505).

HEDYLE (fl. 260's-240's B. C.), Greek poetess, daughter of the poetess Moschine, mother of Hedylus: (27, 53, 67, 68).

HELVIA (fl. 3-43 A. D.), mother of Seneca: (133).

HETAERAE: (92, 116, 152, 168, 170, 175, 182, 193).

HIPPARCHIA (fl. c. 328 B. C.), Greek philosopher, wife of Crates the Cynic, author of many tragedies and philosophical works, none extant: (103).

HONORIA, JUSTA GRATA (c. 418-c. 453 A. D.), daughter of Galla Placidia: (361).

HYPATIA (c. 380-415 A. D.), Alexandrian philosopher and mathematician: (136, 373, 430, 431, 445, 484, 486, 499, 532).

IOTAPE (fl. 33-20 B. C.), princess of Media, daughter of King Artavasdes: (259).

JULIA (c. 83-54 B. C.), virtuous and beautiful daughter of Julius Caesar and wife of Pompey: (385, 410).

JULIA DOMNA (c. 157-217 A. D.), Roman empress, wife of Septimius Severus: (341, 353, 362, 426, 466, 526-528).

JULIA, FLAVIA (c. 65-91 A. D.), daughter of Emperor Titus, mistress of Domitian: (379).

JULIA LIVILLA (18-c. 42 A. D.), daughter of Agrippina the Elder, sister of Caligula, banished for adultery: (396, 397).

JULIA MAESA (d. 226 A. D.), Roman empress, sister of Julia Domna: (341, 362, 466, 525).

JULIA MAJOR (39 B. C. -14 A. D.), daughter of Augustus, banished for adultery: (169, 337, 338, 348, 366, 387, 395-397, 442, 489).

JULIA MAMAEA (d. 235 A. D.), Roman empress, daughter of Julia Maesa, mother of Severus Alexander: (341, 354, 362, 466, 525, 526, 529).

JULIA MINOR (c. 19 B. C. -28 A. D.), daughter of Julia Major, banished likewise for adultery: (396, 397).

JULIA SOAEMIAS (d. 222 A. D.), daughter of Julia Maesa, mother of Elagabalus: (341, 354, 362, 466, 525).

JUNIA (d. 22 A. D.), niece of Cato, sister of Brutus, widow of Cassius: (491).

LAÏS (d. 340 B. C.), celebrated courtesan of Corinth: (150).

LEONTIS (d. c. 110 A. D.), priestess of Delphia: (246).

LESBIA -- see Clodia.

LIVIA DRUSILLA (c. 56 B. C. -29 A. D.), tactful and dignified wife of Augustus: (102, 120, 331, 348, 357, 363, 368, 383, 394, 396, 397, 406, 407, 415, 418, 450, 464, 520, 530, 531).

LOLLIA PAULINA (d. 49 A. D.), third wife of Emperor Caligula: (465).

LUCILLA, ANNA AURELIA GALERIA (c. 148-c. 182 A.D.), daughter of Marcus Aurelius and Faustina the Younger: (339).

LUCRETIA (d. 510 B.C.), legendary Roman matron raped by Sextus, son of Tarquin the Proud: (334).

MAGNIA URBICA (fl. c. 282 A.D.), Roman empress: (478).

MARCELLA CLAUDIA, THE YOUNGER (b. before 40 B.C.), daughter of Augustus' sister Octavia, half-sister to Antonia Major and Minor: (350).

MARCIA (fl. 56-50 B.C.), wife of Cato the Younger and Hortensius: (451).

MARCIA (d. 193 A.D.), concubine of Emperor Commodus: (349).

MARCIANA, ULPIA (c. 48-112 A.D.), sister of Emperor Trajan: (522).

MATIDIA, VIBIA (c. 68-119 A.D.), granddaughter of the above: (522).

MELINNO (fl. 2nd cent. B.C.), poetess, probably from Magnia Graeca, who wrote a five-stanza poem on the power of Rome: (29, 34, 51, 53, 61).

MELISSA (fl. 5th cent. B.C.), Pythagorean philosopher: (48, 57, 64).

MESSALINA, VALERIA (c. 25-48 A.D.), notorious Roman empress, wife of Claudius: (169, 387, 396, 397, 509).

MOERO [MYRO] (fl. c. 300 B.C.), Greek poetess: (44, 45, 53, 55, 67, 68).

MYIA (c. 500 B.C.), Pythagorean philosopher, said to be the daughter of Pythagorus: (48, 57, 64).

MYRTIS (fl. 5th cent. B.C.), Boeotian poetess said to be the teacher of Corinna and Pindar, has no surviving works: (42, 59).

NEAERA (fl. c. 340 B. C.), courtesan of Athens: (106, 107).

NOSSIS (fl. c. 300 B. C.), Greek poetess: (37, 44, 45, 53, 55, 62, 67, 68).

OCTAVIA (c. 69-11 B. C.), sister of Augustus, wife of Mark Antony, beloved for her gentleness and intelligence: (348, 412, 483, 502-504).

OCTAVIA (c. 42-62 A. D.), daughter of Claudius, the mistreated and murdered wife of Nero: (134, 135).

OLYMPIAS (d. 316 B. C.), wife of Philip II of Macedon, mother of Alexander the Great: (261, 262, 307).

ORBIANA (fl. c. 230 A. D.), wife of Emperor Severus Alexander: (525).

PARTHENIS (fl. c. 60 A. D.), Greek poetess of whose works nothing remains: (67, 68).

PAULA, JULIA CORNELIA (m. 219 A. D.), first wife of Emperor Elagabalus: (466, 525).

PAULINA, CAECILIA (fl. 310's A. D.), Roman empress, wife of Maximinus Thrax: (352, 525).

PERICTIONE (fl. c. 5th cent. B. C.), Pythagorean philosopher: (57, 64).

PHILA (c. 350-287 B. C.), daughter of Antipater, wife of King Demetrius of Macedonia: (312).

PHILAENIS (fl. 4th cent. B. C.), Greek poetess: (67, 68).

PHINTYS (fl. c. 5th cent. B. C.), Pythagorean philosopher: (57, 64).

PHRYNE (fl. c. 328 B. C.), Greek courtesan and beauty, model for statues of Aphrodite: (222, 232, 249).

PLAUTILLA (m. 202-d. 212 A. D.), Roman empress, wife of Caracalla: (525).

PLOTINA (d. c. 122 A. D.), wife of Emperor Trajan, noted

for her simple dignity and virtue: (472, 522).

POMPEIA (fl. 67-61 B.C.), third wife of Julius Caesar, whom he divorced because she was not "above suspicion": (385).

POMPONIA (fl. 68-44 B.C.), sister-in-law of Cicero, wife of his brother Quintus: (432).

POPPAEA SABINA, THE YOUNGER (d. 65 A.D.), mistress, then wife, of Nero: (506, 516).

PORCIA (d. 43 B.C.), wife of Brutus, a firm Republican: (459).

PRAXILLA (fl. 451 B.C.), Grecian poetess, wrote dithyrambs, drinking songs, and hymns: (28, 42, 50, 53, 59, 63, 67, 68).

PRIESTESSES: (172, 244, 278, 316, 458, 476).

PROBA, ANICIA FALTONIA (fl. c. 393 A.D.), Roman poetess, a Christian: (71, 73, 80).

PUBLILIA (m. 46 B.C.), second wife of Cicero: (495).

ROXANE (fl. 327 B.C.), Bactrian princess, wife of Alexander the Great: (262).

SABINA, VIBIA (d. c. 136 A.D.), Roman empress, wife of Hadrian, sister of Vibia Matidia: (364, 472, 522).

SABINE WOMEN: (334).

SAPPHO (fl. c. 600 B.C.), great Greek lyric poet: (1-25, 28, 42, 45, 50, 53, 61, 63, 67, 68, 121, 123, 169, 206, 216, 217).

SCRIBONIA (fl. 40 B.C.-16 A.D.), first wife of Augustus, mother of Julia, divorced: (442).

SEMPRONIA (fl. 210's B.C.), daughter of Cornelia, sister of the Gracchi, wife of Scipio Africanus Minor: (375).

SEMPRONIA (fl. 63 B.C.), participant in Catiline's conspiracy: (474).

SERENA (fl. c. 405 A.D.), wife of general Stilicho of the late Eastern Empire: (455).

SERVILIA (fl. 63-44 B.C.), mother of Brutus, mistress of Julius Caesar: (410).

SEVERA, JULIA AQUILIA (m. 220 A.D.), Roman empress, second wife of Elagabalus: (525).

SIBYLS: (69, 81, 83, 84).

SULPICIA (fl. 43 B.C.), Roman poetess, author of six elegies preserved with the works of Tibullus: (70, 72, 76, 86, 87).

SULPICIA (fl. 80 A.D.), Roman poetess, author of love poems and a satire against Domitian: (75, 77, 78, 88, 89).

SULPICIA DRYANTILLA (fl. 210-260 A.D.), wife of Regalianus the governor of Upper Pannonia, who revolted against Gallienus and was briefly proclaimed emperor: (411).

TANAQUIL (fl. c. 616-579 B.C.), Etruscan queen of Rome, wife of Tarquinius Priscus: (320, 321, 368).

TELESILLA (fl. 5th cent. B.C.), Greek poetess: (28, 42, 53, 59, 63).

TERENTIA (fl. 80-44 B.C.), wife of Cicero, Sallust, and Valerius Messalla, lived 103 years: (451, 495, 498).

THAÏS (fl. c. 323 B.C.), Greek courtesan, mistress of Alexander the Great: (268).

THEANO (fl. 540-510 B.C.), Pythagorean philosopher and author, maybe Pythagoras' wife: (42, 48, 57, 64).

TULLIA (c. 79-45 B.C.), Cicero's daughter: (358, 369).

TURIA [THURIA] (fl. 43 B.C.), brave Roman matron, wife of Q. Lucretius Vespillo: (393, 402).

VEGOIA (fl. c. 90 B.C.), Etruscan prophetess: (323).

VESTAL VIRGINS: (357, 419, 429, 492, 493, 497, 517, 533).

VICTORIA [VITRUVIA] (fl. 260's A. D.), Roman empress, mother of Victorinus: (145).

VIRGINIA (d. 449 B. C.), Roman maiden whose murder by her father, in order to save her from the lust of Appius Claudius, prompted the overthrow of the decemvirs: (334, 463).

VIPSANIA AGRIPPINA (d. 20 A. D.), daughter of Caecilia Attica, first wife of Tiberius: (396, 397, 441).

XANTHIPPE (fl. 5th cent. B. C.), wife of Socrates, famed for her shrewishness: (223).

ZENOBIA (fl. 270 A. D.), Queen of Palmyra, challenged Rome in battle: (145, 195, 389, 409, 518, 534).

INDEX OF AUTHORS, EDITORS, AND TRANSLATORS

NOTE: Unless otherwise noted, numbers after the author's name refer to identifying numbers of individual works.